PSYCHED UP

'*Psyched Up* is filled with actionable, practical tips and tools to help reduce anxiety, lower stress and build confidence. McGinn's strategies can create a winning pre-game routine for anyone'
Arianna Huffington

'Daniel McGinn takes readers into locker rooms, backstage on Broadway, on to the sales floor at Yelp and inside the DJ booth at Fenway Park to discover the secrets of how high performers use psychology, superstition and a surprising mix of other tools to get ready for the make-or-break events in their lives. It's a fascinating read'
Charles Duhigg, author of *The Power of Habit* and *Smarter Faster Better*

'Performance anxiety can scuttle great opportunities to showcase your talent and work. *Psyched Up* is an essential user's guide for ensuring you'll be your best when you take centre stage, whether the cameras are rolling or not!'
Katie Couric, journalist and author of *The Best Advice I Ever Got: Lessons from Extraordinary Lives*

'I can't think of another book that's as helpful as this, whether you're shooting a free throw, taking a big test, giving a toast or on one knee proposing. Read *Psyched Up* before your next big moment'
Matt Mullenweg, creator of WordPress and CEO of Automattic

'This book is a gift for entrepreneurs or anyone else who pitches ideas for a living'
Brad Fel   ars

'*Psyched Up* provides a wonderful overview of the science and
practicalities of how to perform well when it matters most.
The book is full of useful takeaways for all of us, including my
favourite, how powerful it can be to have lucky exam shoes'
Gretchen Reynolds, *New York Times* fitness columnist and
author of *The First 20 Minutes*

'A wonderful pleasure to read, *Psyched Up* is an expertly crafted
investigation into the vibrating heart of peak performance'
Po Bronson, author of *Top Dog* and *NurtureShock*

ABOUT THE AUTHOR

Daniel McGinn is an editor at *Harvard Business Review*. His
writing has appeared in *Wired*, *Inc.*, the *Boston Globe Magazine*
and *Newsweek*. He lives in suburban Boston with his family.

PSYCHED UP

HOW THE SCIENCE OF MENTAL PREPARATION
CAN HELP YOU SUCCEED

Daniel McGinn

PORTFOLIO
PENGUIN

PORTFOLIO PENGUIN

UK | USA | Canada | Ireland | Australia
India | New Zealand | South Africa

Portfolio Penguin is part of the Penguin Random House group of companies
whose addresses can be found at global.penguinrandomhouse.com.

First published in the United States of America by Portfolio/Penguin,
an imprint of Penguin Random House LLC 2017
First published in Great Britain by Portfolio 2017
001

Printed in Great Britain by Clays Ltd, St Ives plc

A CIP catalogue record for this book is available from the British Library

ISBN: 978–0–241–31052–6

www.greenpenguin.co.uk

MIX
Paper from
responsible sources
FSC
www.fsc.org   FSC® C018179

Penguin Random House is committed to a
sustainable future for our business, our readers
and our planet. This book is made from Forest
Stewardship Council® certified paper.

For Abby, Jack, and Tommy

Contents

INTRODUCTION

Just after 8 A.M. on a summer morning, Mark McLaughlin is sprawled on a ratty armchair that he's shoved into a dark corner of a hospital locker room in central New Jersey. In a few moments, McLaughlin, who is a neurosurgeon, will make a six-inch incision into the back of a seventy-three-year-old patient whose arthritis has caused the lower part of his spinal nerve to crimp, threatening his ability to walk. The operation will take more than three hours. McLaughlin will be drilling, chipping, and cutting amid vital nerves, just inches from the patient's aorta. McLaughlin needs to be focused.

Clad in green surgical scrubs, McLaughlin lays his feet out on a low table and reclines. His eyes are closed. His iPhone sits on his chest, playing a Bach cantata at low volume. For a few minutes, he sits in silence. When the patient is anesthetized, the nurse calls his phone to signal him. Then McLaughlin—who is fifty-one, wears glasses, has graying hair, and retains the broad, muscled back of a former college wrestler—gets up and walks briskly toward the operating room down the hall.

Most surgeons work very differently than McLaughlin does. In the moments before an operation, they chat and joke with nurses and colleagues. They check e-mail, do paperwork, and make phone calls. They are relaxed and nonchalant, treating surgery as just an ordinary part of their workday.

McLaughlin doesn't banter. As he scrubs his hands at the sink, a lead-lined apron now over his scrubs to protect him from the X-rays used during surgery, his eyes are again closed. If a colleague tries to talk to him, McLaughlin replies a bit rudely: "Not now." He's engaged in his presurgical routine, which evolved from a practice he first learned to use in the wrestling room of a New Jersey prep school, an hour's drive from the hospital where he now operates.

McLaughlin began wrestling in sixth grade, and although he immediately showed a talent for the sport, his physical skills only took him so far. Over time he identified what was holding him back. "Physically, I was completely prepared," he says. "Mentally, I wasn't."

So McLaughlin began working with a sports psychologist, who helped him create a highly choreographed routine of mental preparation. Before matches McLaughlin would visualize a Greatest Hits reel of his best wrestling moments, reinforcing his confidence. "The psychologist taught me to remember the sights and sounds of positive events—the feeling of the mat, what was around me, the colors," he recalls. "We focused the preliminary routine to try to get me into that autopilot mode and let my body fall into that groove."

After he began using this prematch routine, McLaughlin's experience on the mat changed. He no longer heard the crowd. His sense of time was altered. Though wrestling matches last six minutes, it felt as if they ended after thirty seconds. The worries, self-doubts, and negative thoughts decreased dramatically. And he began winning most of his matches.

McLaughlin went on to wrestle at William & Mary, where he was team captain (twice), won the Virginia state championship, and was inducted into the college's athletic Hall of Fame. Then he attended medical school, eventually specializing in neurosurgery.

A few years later, as a surgical fellow, McLaughlin began to recognize similarities between the stresses of wrestling and the pressures of surgery. As a surgeon, he has to stay hyperfocused; if his attention wanders, something bad could happen very quickly—just as it could, albeit with lower stakes, in wrestling. As a surgeon, he achieves a positive or negative result, and over time his reputation depends on his win-loss record—just as it had in wrestling.

So before every operation, he began utilizing the techniques that made such a difference in his wrestling career, by going through a systematic, ritualized process to put his mind in the optimal state.

The routine began early this morning, when McLaughlin drank the first of the three cups of coffee he consumes before entering the operating room. If he's awakened late at night while on call to do emergency surgery, he may drink even more, especially if it looks like a long procedure. (McLaughlin's longest operation lasted eighteen hours.) To stay attentive during long periods with limited sleep, some surgeons rely on a prescription medication called Provigil, a "wakefulness-promoting" drug that allows users to stay awake and focused for twenty-four to thirty-six hours. (It's also used by truck drivers, entrepreneurs, and Wall Street traders.) Some surgeons and dentists also rely on beta blockers to steady hands during procedures that make them especially anxious. McLaughlin has never suffered from uncontrollable tremors, and he's tried Provigil but doesn't like it; it makes him paranoid. So he relies on coffee as his sole presurgical chemical aid. "I strongly believe caffeine is a performance enhancer," he says. "When I'm operating, I'm a really good concentrator, and I have no doubt caffeine adds to that."

As he moves from the cafeteria to the locker room and then into the surgical wing, McLaughlin is engaged in the next step in his process: running through a precise series of thoughts and visualizations, which he calls the Five Ps. First is a Pause: He tries to forget what's happened earlier in the day and focus only on the present. Next he thinks deeply about the Patient. "This is a seventy-three-year-old man, and this is the most important moment of his life. We need him to come out of this pain free and able to walk more easily," he says to himself. He reviews his Plan, mentally rehearsing the surgery step-by-step. Then he offers some Positive thoughts: "You were put on this earth to do this operation," he says. "It's such a privilege to be able to use your skills to help this patient." Finally, as he steps toward the table, he says a quick Prayer. "It's very ritualistic, and I'm very focused," he says.

Before a routine elective procedure like this one, McLaughlin doesn't say much to the surgical team as they gather around the operating table. But in certain situations, especially when confronting a fast-moving trauma case, McLaughlin uses another pre-performance technique: He gives his colleagues a pep talk. "Listen, we have to pull together," he will say. "This patient is dying. We have ten minutes. Let's be a team. Help one another. Stay focused on what needs to be done. Don't get frustrated." If he gave these talks before every case, they would probably lose their power. However, since he uses them only in extreme situations, McLaughlin believes his words help the group perform at its best.

Like most surgeons, McLaughlin plays music before and during an operation. Unlike most doctors, he has extremely specific preferences based on the type of procedure he's doing. Most of his playlists consist of country music. During especially stressful operations, he turns on a classical mix, which calms him. When a patient is bleeding excessively, he'll ask to hear some George Strait. For reasons he can't explain, it helps him staunch the flow. And when a surgery gets particularly challenging, he plays John Hiatt's inspirational country song "Through Your Hands." "It sounds crazy, but when I'm struggling, it helps me get through," he says. The song is so meaningful that McLaughlin hired Hiatt to play at his fiftieth birthday party.

Some parts of McLaughlin's presurgical ritual don't make much sense, and if you don't know their significance, you wouldn't readily recognize why he does them. For instance, just before this operation begins, he injects 19 milliliters of lidocaine into the site of the incision. Most surgeons would use a round number such as 20 milliliters, but McLaughlin prefers dosages that end in 9s, which he considers a lucky number. And in a surgical tray nearby, he keeps a set of microsurgical tools called Jannetta instruments, named after the renowned neurosurgeon Peter Jannetta, who was McLaughlin's mentor. The tools are obsolete now—McLaughlin rarely uses them—but he finds their presence comforting in a superstitious sort of way. "It's kind of like having Dr. Jannetta in the room with me when I do hard cases," he says. "When they aren't there, I get anxious."

While McLaughlin typically exudes a calm confidence before he operates, occasionally he'll display a flash of anger—not unlike the hostility he used to feel for his opponent before wrestling matches. "My opponent is the disease I'm operating on, and I think about it as an adversary," he says. "It's not driven by hatred. It's more of an intellectual process of 'How am I going to defeat this thing?'" Occasionally he'll trash-talk his clinical opponent during the procedure, muttering: "I'm gonna kick your ass."

There are downsides to McLaughlin's regimen. By multitasking right up until the moment they make the first incision, other surgeons can be more productive, attending to administrative duties. And because McLaughlin is so silent and focused before he begins his work, the atmosphere in his operating room feels slightly tense; if I were a nurse, I might prefer working in an OR where coworkers chat about last night's TV show or discuss plans for the coming weekend.

McLaughlin admits there is no hard proof that the things he does in the moments before operating increase his performance, nor is there an easy way to test whether they make a difference. But he believes his routine boosts his focus and concentration when it matters most, reducing the odds he'll make a mistake. And even if the atmosphere is serious, he thinks colleagues appreciate the fact that his work habits are steady and predictable. "I can't produce any evidence," he says. "I think my routine helps, but I don't really know."

Unlike Mark McLaughlin, I was a mediocre high school athlete. Scrawny and slow, I was a second-string offensive lineman on the football team; my biggest fan was the team's laundress, since my game uniform rarely got dirty. In basketball, after some success in ninth and tenth grades, everyone else got taller and I became a guard with limited ball-handling skills. By the time I reached the varsity level in both sports, I served a function similar to that of the legendary Celtics' coach Red Auerbach's cigar: If I entered the game, it signaled that my coach felt victory was safely in hand.

Still, high school sports gave me a window into the psychological techniques coaches used to prepare us (and the players used to prepare themselves) in the final moments before a game. Like most teams, ours relied on specific music to rev us up; when I hear those songs thirty years later, my pulse still quickens. Our teams had ritualistic pregame prayers and routines. The coaches worked to kindle a sense of hostility toward key rivals. We spent hours listening to pep talks aimed at instilling a sense of purpose.

I came away with a lifelong fascination with how people get psyched up before important events. When I watch the Olympics, I'm as interested in what the athletes do *before* a race as I am in the race itself. I'm drawn to political photography that captures candidates just before they walk onto a debate stage or give a make-or-break speech. How do they stay calm? What tools boost their confidence? What mental tricks optimize their performance?

As an adult, my job couldn't be less athletic. As an editor at *Harvard Business Review,* I spend my days reading academic research and helping professors, consultants, and executives write articles that aim to "improve the practice of management"—our company's mission. It's a great job, but not one that inspires high-fiving or dumping Gatorade on the boss's head.

Yet as I sift through research, I am surprised by how frequently I come across experiments involving variations of the practices I experienced in the high school locker room. I routinely discover academic studies that examine how people use self-talk and pep talks, rituals and superstition, mental tricks and other gambits to prepare for the high-pressure tasks of a white-collar professional. In many cases, evidence shows that these routines really do help people perform better.

Some of these ideas, such as Harvard professor Amy Cuddy's celebrated (and controversial) work on "power posing," have made their way into the mainstream. But much of this research remains obscure.

In the years since Malcolm Gladwell published *Outliers,* we've become a society obsessed with practice, with systematically grinding our way to the magical 10,000 hours required for proficiency. Practice is vital to any high performer, of course, but eventually you run out of rehearsal time. The audience is seated and the orchestra is warmed up, or the patient is anesthetized and the nurse is handing you the scalpel. Whether the performance takes place in a courtroom, a classroom, or a boardroom, and whether it involves a presentation, a negotiation, a sales pitch, or a job interview, we have just a few moments to collect our thoughts and prepare our minds. There's no room for more practice. We need quick-hit tactics and life hacks. In fact, there's a growing body of research on how best to spend those crucial moments. But just like the surgeons Mark McLaughlin observes, most of us ignore these techniques and just jump in.

Psyched Up is a book about what to do in these vital moments just before you perform. We'll examine new ways to deal with the flood of adrenaline, increase focus, boost confidence, and otherwise optimize our emotions before we take the stage. We'll explore how music can (and sometimes can't) help people do better, whether focusing on a rival can lead to improvement, and what kinds of pep talks work best. We'll also meet high-performing professionals who are putting these techniques to work. We'll look at the mental preparation of athletes, actors, musicians, soldiers, salespeople, and others who, despite years of practice and enviable track records, will ultimately be judged on their ability to deliver a single solid performance when it counts.

Most of what we know about the process of getting psyched up comes from sports. We learned it in locker rooms from well-meaning coaches, and it's based largely on intuition or common sense. But as psychologists and social scientists have begun taking closer looks at what really helps put our minds and emotions in an optimal state before we perform, they're finding that our intuition often betrays us. Some of the advice is conflicting. Many of us end up doing the wrong things. You really can get better results with a better set of practices, and chances are, they're not what you're doing now.

Many of us can profit from a better pre-performance routine. As the nature of work has changed, many professionals' success or failure is now less dependent on repetitive daily tasks and instead based on a thin slice of evaluative moments. Working on projects involves more crucial first impressions, followed by more final presentations. Self-employment and the "gigs" and "side hustles" of modern life require people to interview for jobs or sell their services more frequently. Think of it as the "Shark Tank economy," in which we have more riding on the ability to deliver a pitch under pressure. If you work two thousand hours a year but your overall success rests mostly on your performance during a couple of dozen crucial hours—at pitch meetings, sales calls, a key conversation with your boss, and so on—the tools in this book should help you do better.

Back in the operating room, it's nearing lunchtime as Mark McLaughlin finishes tying a long series of internal stitches and hands the surgical needle to his assistant, who will finish closing. He heads back to the locker room, changes into khakis and a polo shirt, and walks to the waiting area. "Everything went really well. He should be able to go home in two or three days," he tells the patient's wife. She asks if her husband will be able to walk easily again, and McLaughlin says it looks very good.

Another surgeon—one who was tweeting or joking around before picking up the scalpel—may well have obtained a similar outcome. But if it was your loved one on the table, wouldn't it be reassuring to know that in the final moments before the doctor performed, he was doing everything he could to increase the odds?

This book will show you how to do it.

Chapter One

FIGHTING BACK AGAINST FIGHT OR FLIGHT

---

*SHOULD YOU "CALM DOWN" OR JUST
EMBRACE THE ADRENALINE RUSH?*

When Noa Kageyama was seven years old, he attended a summer music program at Ithaca College, and like most music camps, this one culminated in a recital. Kageyama, who was raised in central Ohio, had begun playing violin at age two. At five, he'd traveled to Japan to study with Shinichi Suzuki, creator of the famed Suzuki method of music instruction. By six, he'd played his violin on television. So by the time he was seven, Kageyama was a seasoned performer. As he stood waiting to go on stage, he felt relaxed and at ease. What could possibly go wrong?

Then, a few moments before his turn, a young female violinist took the stage and had a meltdown. She kept stopping and starting, as if she were forgetting the song. The distress on her face was obvious, and watching from a few feet away, Kageyama experienced an epiphany—one that would change the course of his life.

"The whole concept that something bad could happen on stage popped into my awareness. I didn't know that could happen, because I'd never seen that before," he says. As he waited to play, Kageyama began to feel this strange mix of feelings, a kind of apprehensiveness that was so unfamiliar he didn't even know what to call it.

Despite this nascent anxiety, Kageyama performed just fine at the Ithaca recital. Afterward, he kept practicing the violin every day. As a teenager, he played with adult symphonies, won fellowships, and studied with world-famous violinists. During his senior year of high school, each weekend he would fly from Ohio to New York City, to participate in a precollege program at the Juilliard School. Along the way, he never experienced a full-blown panic while performing.

Still, he did experience subtle signs of anxiety. Sometimes his hands would sweat excessively. Sometimes his mind would wander. "There was this frustration over why I couldn't consistently play the way I was capable of playing, even if I was prepared," he says. Although his performance anxiety was not particularly noticeable to observers, he began to see it as an unpredictable, pernicious tax that unjustly subtracted from the expected return on the time he'd spent practicing.

In 1999, as a twenty-three-year-old a graduate student at Juilliard, Kageyama signed up for an elective class called "Performance

Enhancement for Musicians," taught by a sports psychologist who'd previously worked with Olympic athletes. The course taught him that backstage jitters are an unavoidable part of a musician's life, and that even if you can't entirely eliminate them, you can systematically develop skills to perform well despite them. "It was such an eye-opener," Kageyama says. "It's not a crapshoot out there. There are things I could do to get better at this."

The course had an unintended consequence: It led him to quit playing violin altogether. As an undergrad, Kageyama had majored in psychology, and the more the young violinist considered what really interested him, the more he realized he wanted to teach people the skills he'd learned in the Juilliard course, rather than play music himself. So after graduating from Juilliard's master's program, he moved to Indiana University to pursue a PhD in psychology. Today his violin sits in a case that is rarely opened.

Instead, at 11 A.M. on a September morning, Professor Kageyama stands in Room 102 at Juilliard, teaching a new version of the course that changed his life. Kageyama is thin and soft spoken, with close-trimmed black hair. Around him in a circle of chairs are twenty grad students, instrument cases—violas, cellos, flutes, bassoons—at their feet. The previous week, in the semester's first class, he'd made the students take their instruments, one by one, to the front of the room while he fiddled with a video recorder set up on a tripod. (He didn't actually record the performances. He used the camera, and told students he would send the videos to Juilliard's dean, to increase their stress levels.) He told each student to play for sixty seconds, but then actually set a timer for ninety seconds, to flummox them. He wanted to see them play under pressure.

In this week's class, he alternates between lecture and discussion, focusing on how adrenaline and the body's physiological fight-or-flight response can have particularly detrimental effects on musicians. Pianists' fingers will go cold; shallow breathing and dry mouth can wreak havoc on musicians playing wind instruments. To help these students learn to cope better with these phenomena, Kageyama leads them through a relaxation exercise called centering, and then schedules appointments with each student to go over their individual results from an 84-question Performance Skill Inventory, which highlights each musician's particular strengths and weaknesses in dealing with performance anxiety.

As Kageyama and I exit the classroom and walk uptown to a Chinese restaurant, he tells me his plans for next week's class: He's going to make the musicians do calisthenics until their hearts are racing and their bodies are sweaty, and then have them play their instrument. "It's distracting when your heart is pounding," he says, but if you practice playing while feeling that sensation, it can become a little less unnerving. "It's the same thing you need in an audition—to see past what your body is saying, and to focus on the task at hand."

Kageyama compares a musician facing an audition to a rocket that's poised on the launch pad, experiencing the ticktock of the countdown. Rather than experience this countdown passively, he wants students to practice specific steps to get them ready to launch. The ultimate goal of his fifteen-week course, he says, is "to ensure that, in those last few seconds, you're set up as best you can to be successful."

2.

In helping humans perform, psychology is the software, but biology is the hardware. Much of what performance psychologists like Noa Kageyama do is help people control and adjust to the chemical processes happening inside their bodies—and the emotional responses they create—when they're getting ready to perform.

These processes primarily involve the hormone adrenaline and the emotion of anxiety. Finding ways to control this biological and emotional response is the first step in making better use of the countdown period Kagayama describes.

Doctors first identified the adrenals, the small organs attached to the top of the kidneys, in the sixteenth century, but it took anatomists three hundred years to figure out what purpose they served. By the mid-1800s, doctors began seeing a pattern in patients with tumors on these organs: When the adrenals weren't working well, patients suffered from low blood pressure, fatigue, and fainting. In the 1890s, doctors began injecting adrenaline, which they extracted from adrenals, into animals (and a few humans) and observing how this mysterious substance resulted in instantaneous jumps in blood pressure, heart rate, and respiration.

In one 1903 experiment reported by the *New York Times,* a researcher used anesthetics to stop a dog's heartbeat, rendering it lifeless for fifteen minutes, and then revived the animal with a shot of adrenaline. Afterward, the researcher was besieged with letters asking if he could use the hormone to perform Lazarus-like revivals of people who'd been dead for years.

Although adrenaline isn't that miraculous, scientists immediately marveled at its adaptive utility. "When a person is, say, running from a ferocious dog, [adrenaline] changes and integrates the function of organs in favorable ways," writes Harvard Medical School professor Brian B. Hoffman in *Adrenaline,* his fascinating history of the hormone. "It increases the output of the heart in order to pump more oxygen-rich blood full of nutrients to the rest of the body; increases blood flow to the muscles and away from other organs where it is not immediately needed, such as the intestines; opens the lungs to breathe in more oxygen; and cuts blood flow to the skin to limit bleeding in case of injury." By the 1920s, the Harvard physiologist Walter Cannon had coined a name for the distinctive set of reactions this system creates in response to stress: "fight or flight."

Stage fright is just one peculiar manifestation of fight or flight, but it's such a familiar and widespread phenomenon that it's been deeply researched. That makes it particularly useful in trying to understand what works and what doesn't in trying to manage adrenaline and anxiety.

Although most of us are not concert musicians, a surprising amount of the research done on stage fright focuses on this profession. That's mostly because performing as a concert musician is *really* hard, especially when compared with giving a TED Talk or a boardroom presentation, or appearing on television. "With public speaking, there's a lot of wiggle room. The audience doesn't know what you're supposed to say," Kageyama says. "There's a lot of improvisation going on in a presentation, but in music, everybody knows what note is supposed to come next, and how it's supposed to sound." There's also insane competition: A big-city symphony may audition two hundred musicians for the single opening.

If you dive deeply into research on stage fright, the most striking aspect is the pervasiveness of the problem. In *Playing Scared: A History and Memoir of Stage Fright,* the journalist and amateur pianist Sara Solovitch tallies up the musicians (including Paul McCartney, Vladimir Horowitz, Ella Fitzgerald, Luciano

Pavarotti, Rod Stewart, Bette Midler, and Barbra Streisand) who've struggled with severe onstage anxiety. Solovitch describes stage fright as "both utterly mysterious, an act of mutiny by the mind against the body, and ludicrously commonplace, as ordinary as the common cold." She goes on to list the techniques—including hypnosis, meditation, yoga, cognitive behavior therapy, psycho-pharmaceuticals, exposure therapy, eye movement therapy, and various breathing exercises—she sampled to overcome her fears and perform a piano recital.

Some performers develop creative techniques for dealing with the affliction. Carly Simon is an extreme and oft-noted example. In 1981, during a concert in Pittsburgh, Simon suffered an onstage anxiety attack so profound that she asked audience members to climb on stage to rub her arms to help calm her down, allowing her to finish the show. (She describes the incident in detail in her 2015 memoir, *Boys in the Trees*.) The episode caused her to cancel a tour, and she didn't sing again in public for seven years. "It's terribly paradoxical, because I do enjoy [performing]. But when the anxiety comes on, the adrenaline is so strong it topples me," she recalled later. Over time, Simon began instructing theaters to turn on the houselights, to reduce the spotlight's focus on her. She would focus obsessively on a single spectator in the front rows, intending to make this fan feel embarrassed by the attention, pushing that emotion away from herself. In the 1990s, she began bringing a couch on stage so she could sing lying down.

When she learned that physical pain could reduce her emotional anxiety, she began jabbing her hand with pins while on stage, or asking to be spanked before the show began. John Lahr, writing in the *New Yorker,* recounts how at a 1996 birthday performance for President Clinton, the curtain very nearly went up while Simon was being spanked on stage by the entire horn section of her band.

Alas, Simon's prescription notwithstanding, there is no academic research suggesting that pre-performance spanking can help large numbers of people beat back pre-performance jitters. But there is surprising research that suggests that the most common advice that's given to people who are nervous before a performance—to try to relax and calm down—usually does more harm than good.

3.

As a freshman at Princeton, Alison Wood Brooks auditioned for a coed a cappella singing group called the Princeton Roaring 20. Gaining a spot in the group is hypercompetitive: Each year, approximately a hundred students try out for the three or four spots left open by graduating seniors. Although she had no formal singing experience—she'd played oboe and piano in high school—Brooks had a splendid voice. So on a fall evening, she confidently walked into the audition room and sang "Beautiful" by Christina

Aguilera. "It was exactly like something out of *Pitch Perfect*," she says. A few nights later, Brooks was invited the join the group.

Once she did, she became one of the judges at future auditions. During her sophomore, junior, and senior years, as Brooks watched several hundred candidates go through the tryout ordeal, she began to notice two distinct types of behavior. One group of singers would be visibly nervous before they sang. Their voices or their bodies might tremble slightly. Some might even apologize before they started singing: "I'm sorry. I'm really nervous." A second group of singers acted differently. They seemed more positively energized and less uncomfortable. They tended to smile and talk about being excited rather than anxious. "I really appreciate the opportunity," they'd say sincerely.

As Brooks watched the divergent behavior, she noticed a trend in how they performed. "The people who seemed to do well in the audition reframed their anxiety as excitement, or channeled it in a positive direction," she says. The visibly nervous singers generally didn't sing as well.

After graduating from Princeton, Brooks entered a doctoral program at the University of Pennsylvania's Wharton School. In the evenings she began watching *American Idol*, and as she watched the early-season auditions, she observed behavior that mirrored what she saw at the Roaring 20 auditions. Contestants who talked about being nervous during preaudition interviews with Ryan Seacrest tended to do poorly in front of the judges, while people who expressed excitement often performed better.

As a grad student, Brooks became interested in how different emotions affect people's performance in various kinds of tasks. Her primary interest: anxiety. "Researchers have been interested in and aware of anxiety issues, at least at a clinical level, for a very long time, but what we don't know a lot about is the anxiety that normal people feel every day," she says. Brooks is talking about the difference between "trait" anxiety, the individual quality that may make someone susceptible to an anxiety disorder that requires medicine or treatment, and "state" anxiety, which describes how well-balanced people with no particular susceptibility to anxiety react to a stressful situation.

As a doctoral student, Brooks coauthored papers that examined how people negotiate while feeling anxious (they generally do poorly), and how people who are anxious become overly dependent on advisers or experts when making decisions. Her research utilizes unique methods to make people feel anxious: In one set of experiments, she had subjects listen to the music from *Psycho* and watch clips of horror movies before they engaged in tasks.

For her dissertation, she set up a scientific experiment to test out the phenomenon she first noticed while judging auditions for the Princeton Roaring 20. First she tried to understand how frequently people think that "calming down" is the best way to deal with a performance situation. She surveyed two hundred people about what they'd tell a nervous coworker who's about to give a big speech. More than 90 percent of participants would tell the friend to "try to relax and calm down," while just under 8 percent would advise to "try to be excited instead of anxious." In her dissertation, she references the British wartime poster with the motto "Keep Calm and Carry On." For people facing stressful situations, this is the ubiquitous advice.

For the second part of her study, she recruited 113 people to sing the Journey song "Don't Stop Believin'," using the Nintendo Wii game Karaoke Revolution, with the computer program giving each singer a score based on pitch and rhythm. The singers were randomly divided into three groups, and just before each person began singing, he or she was instructed to do one of three things. One group said nothing. One group said aloud: "I'm so anxious." The third group said: "I'm so excited." When the scores were tallied, the Nintendo system gave the "I'm so excited" singers an average score of 80.52 percent. The singers who'd said nothing scored 69.27 percent. The performers who'd said they were anxious scored 52.98 percent. In two follow-up experiments—one that required people to give a work-related speech, and another that required people to do difficult math problems—she again found that people who talked about being "excited" just before the task significantly outperformed people who talked about being nervous, or calm, or were told to try to remain calm.

"People have this really strong intuition to try to calm down in stressful situations," says Brooks, a dark-haired and vivacious assistant professor at Harvard Business School who works from an office above the school's library. "You hear it all the time. People either actively say, 'Calm down,' or they say, 'Don't be anxious.' The hitch is that it seems quite difficult to find strategies to actually do that."

The psychological term for the process Brooks's work describes is "reappraisal," and it describes how someone can reevaluate a potentially emotion-eliciting situation in a way that changes its emotional impact. It's one of a group of strategies that are part of the process known as emotion regulation. James Gross, a Stanford psychologist who's the preeminent authority on emotion regulation, describes a variety of tactics people can use to regulate their emotions. For instance, "situation selection" refers to one's ability to avoid the circumstances that might lead to anger or sadness or anxiety. (If your child freaks out around clowns, for instance, you might avoid circuses.) "Situation modification" describes methods to alter the environment to reduce negative emotions. (When Carly Simon orders the houselights on at her shows, she's using this strategy.) "Attentional deployment" refers to ways to make someone less aware of the circumstances that spark a negative emotion. (Distraction is one example.) Reappraisal is an example of a tactic that Gross calls "cognitive change," in which you don't actually change the surroundings that are causing negative emotions, but instead try to alter your under-standing of the circumstances.

In a perfect world, it might be possible to reappraise one's feelings of nervousness into an unaroused, nonchalant calm. Brooks suggests that in reality, that's too great a leap. "The argu-ment is that anxiety and excitement are actually very, very close, but that anxiety and calmness are too far apart," she says. So in-stead of aiming for calm, the smarter strategy is to force yourself to make the more subtle, achievable mental shift from nervousness to excitement.

Compared with most areas of psychology, reappraisal is a rel-atively new field of study. But Brooks isn't the only researcher do-ing experiments to try to better understand its power. University of Rochester professor Jeremy Jamieson has done a series of stud-ies on reappraisal, many of them examining how students can use it while taking exams. For instance, in a 2010 study, Jamieson and colleagues looked at a group of students taking practice exams to prepare for the GRE, a standardized test for grad school admis-sions. Just before the exam, they read one group of test takers the following statement:

People think that feeling anxious while taking a standard-ized test will make them do poorly on the test. However, re-cent research suggests that arousal doesn't hurt performance on these tests and can even help performance . . . This means that you shouldn't feel concerned if you do feel anxious while taking today's GRE test. If you find yourself feeling anxious, simply remind yourself that your arousal could be helping you do well.

When they looked at the test results, the researchers found no difference in the verbal scores between people who read that statement and people who didn't. However, on the math exam, people who'd read the reappraisal statement scored, on average, 55 points higher—a significant jump. When they followed up to see how the students fared on the actual GRE more than a month later, they found that despite the elapsed time, the students who'd read the reappraisal statement during the experiment scored 65 points higher in math, had worried less about feeling anxious, and still believed that anxiety would help their performance.

Jamieson and his colleagues concluded: "People's appraisals of their internal states are flexible, [and] the manner in which internal states are interpreted can have profound effects on emotion, physiology, and behavior."

For people who suffer from extreme nerves before a performance, the takeaway from the reappraisal research is clear: No matter what anyone tells you, don't obsess over calming down. Instead, tell yourself the sweaty palms and racing heart are a positive sign, because they signify excitement. You're lucky to be here and to have this opportunity to prove how good you are. Instead of Journey, try to channel the Pointer Sisters, and quietly hum to yourself: "I'm so excited, and I just can't hide it. . . . "

4.

When I began reporting this book, I held a simplistic view of getting psyched, one that was overly focused on adrenaline and arousal. I thought that getting psyched was akin to flipping an on-off switch. For an energetic, aggressive activity, more adrenaline is obviously better, so psyching up consists of finding ways, such as the right kind of music, to flip the switch on, I thought. For other, quieter activities—a piano recital, an archery tournament, or a job interview—arousal will translate into jitteriness or distraction. So preparing to perform consists largely of trying to turn the adrenaline switch off.

The reality, according to research that stretches back more than a century, is far more nuanced. Much of it seems to affirm Alison Wood Brooks's contention that striving to be calm isn't necessarily a performer's best bet.

In 1908, a pair of Harvard psychologists named Robert Yerkes and John Dodson were conducting a complicated set of learning experiments in which they administered electric shocks to a hyperactive species of mouse, and then observed how quickly the mice learned to navigate through a mazelike contraption. In general terms, they found that the mice learned more quickly when given a medium-sized shock, and performed poorly when the shock was either too low or too high. The experiments didn't involve humans and weren't designed to study the effects of what we now think of as performance anxiety, and more recent academics have challenged their conclusions. Nonetheless, the results came to be celebrated as the Yerkes-Dodson Law, which is still featured in basic psychology textbooks. The law describes the curvilinear relationship between anxiety (or stress) and performance. People perform best not when they're totally calm, and not when they're totally stressed, but somewhere in the middle.

Academic theory notwithstanding, the idea caught on because it makes a lot of sense. Playing quarterback in the Super Bowl and defending a doctoral thesis are entirely different kinds of performances, and it's true that a football player may seek to intentionally elevate his arousal while the PhD aspirant may try to quell her nerves. But in each case, there are limits: Even the PhD student shouldn't aim for total calm or complete relaxation, and the quarterback will make bad decisions if he's too amped up. Some level of nervous energy is good. That optimal level will vary among different kinds of people and the task at hand. Getting psyched up isn't really an on-off switch, but more of a volume knob; the ideal level of arousal falls somewhere on a continuum, and skilled performers twist the volume up or down depending on the context of their performance, in an attempt to find the sweet spot.

While the Yerkes-Dodson Law continues to hold some sway, the newer theory about how performers manage arousal and emotions comes from a Finnish sports psychologist named Yuri Hanin, who first devised it while working with Finnish and Russian divers, gymnasts, rowers, and swimmers in the 1970s. These athletes' experience defied the Yerkes-Dodson model: Many performed well at extremely high stress levels, beyond what the curvilinear model might suggest. Hanin also recognized that stress or anxiety wasn't the only emotion they were feeling. They also felt happiness, sadness, anger, fear, and a myriad of other emotions. So Hanin proposed a model called the Individualized Zones of Optimal Functioning, or IZOF. The model recognizes that athletes feel a variety of emotions before competing, and that the optimal level of emotions can vary dramatically from one athlete to another—and even for a single athlete, it might vary based on the context of a particular competition. Over the last thirty-five years, Hanin has used this model to try to help athletes retrospectively analyze what emotions they were feeling before good or bad performances, and then create a prescriptive model of how they want to feel before an event. The athlete then works, in the days, hours, and minutes before performing, to raise or lower the emotions to put herself in the optimal zones.

Instead of an on-off switch or a volume knob, the IZOF model imagines something more like the mixing board in a recording studio, allowing a user to fine-tune different emotions in varying quantities to try to find an optimal blend.

The other technique that sports psychologists teach to try to help performers manage energy and arousal in the moments before a performance is called centering—the technique Noa Kageyama teaches his classes at Juilliard. The technique was devised by Robert Nideffer, who'd gone to Japan to study the martial art of aikido in the early 1960s and became fascinated by the calm and focused demeanor of the best aikido practitioners. He returned to the United States to earn a doctorate in psychology and became a prominent sports psychologist in the 1970s; in the process, he devised a way for athletes to calm themselves before a performance. Nideffer taught the process to a protégé named Don Greene, a West Point grad and former Green Beret who popularized the practice.

For his doctoral dissertation, Greene worked with the San Diego SWAT team. Before the SWAT team engaged in live-fire drills, Greene had half the shooters perform the centering exercise, and the other half do nothing. The centered shooters performed significantly better, clearing an alley more quickly and shooting more bad guys (and fewer good guys) than the control group. Greene later used the technique with Olympians, Wall

Street traders, and disparate other professionals. He taught the 1999 class at Juilliard that changed Noa Kageyama's career path.

Centering involves a seven-step process, which I'll describe briefly. (The description that follows is drawn from Don Greene's book *Fight Your Fear and Win*.) It sounds a lot like mindfulness or meditation, but there's at least one key difference: Greene insists that with proper practice, someone can center himself in less than ten seconds.

1. **Form your clear intention:** Clear the jumble of thoughts by focusing on just a single aim, such as "I'm going to convince this buyer to sign a contract." Don't waffle, and keep the goal positive.

2. **Pick a focal point:** Aim your eyes at an unimportant distant point, toward which you're later going to mentally fling excess energy, stress, and nervousness.

3. **Breathe mindfully:** Close your eyes, breathe in through your nose and out through your mouth, and fully expand your belly with each breath.

4. **Release muscle tension:** Progressively relax your muscles, starting at your head and moving down your body, checking one area per inhale.

5. **Find your center:** Think about a spot two inches below your navel and two inches below the surface of your belly. That's your center. Focusing on this spot quiets your mind.

6. **Repeat your process cue:** This is a phrase that's supposed to trigger a specific action that gets you toward your intention. For a golfer, it might be "smooth, good tempo"; for a negotiator, it might be "ask questions and be friendly."

7. **Direct your energy:** Hurl excess energy at the focal point you identified in step 2.

I've read longer versions of centering, and it seems like a technique that's difficult to learn from reading about it; like meditation, yoga, or a golf swing, it will be easier to learn if someone who really understands how to do it teaches it to you directly.

On the surface, centering appears analogous to "calming down." If that's true, it may seem to be in opposition to Alison Wood Brooks's finding that trying to "calm down" can hurt performance. There's an explanation for that divergence, however. Centering is a *systematic* way to try to calm down, one that forces the user to go through specific steps that also occupy the mind, distracting a performer from whatever nervousness she might be feeling. Brooks's subjects see their performance deteriorate when they *try* to be calm without having real tools to accomplish that; Don Greene's centering practitioners know exactly *how* to turn down the dials in their body, which makes a difference.

Based on a written description, centering doesn't sound like a life-changing technique, but I've met people who say it's absolutely changed the way they spend the final moments before a performance. Greene writes: "The whole idea behind finding your center is to feel rooted, grounded, stabilized—and in control of your energy."

5.

In the penultimate week of Professor Kageyama's "Performance Enhancement for Musicians" class at Juilliard, he prepares his students for the mock audition that will take place during the final class. This evaluation, according to the syllabus, will account for 50 percent of their final grade.

Kageyama shows students the third-floor rehearsal space where they can relax and do some last-minute practice before they enter the audition room. In the audition room itself, he shows them the screen that separates the musician from the judges, giving the performer a sense of anonymity. Screened auditions are the norm in many music auditions; research shows that screens help judges make their evaluations based solely on the music, limiting the potential for bias due to gender, ethnicity, or other visible attributes. He tells the students they will be evaluated by a three-judge panel consisting of Juilliard faculty members and outside musicians from the New York City Ballet, the Metropolitan Opera, or the New York Philharmonic. Then he has each student play his or her audition piece in front of the class.

One week later, when the students show up for the mock audition, the process doesn't go as smoothly as Kageyama had promised. In fact, nearly everything he's told them to expect turns out to be a lie.

Instead of being called upstairs to perform in a precise order, the students are called up randomly and without warning. Kageyama instructs them to take the stairs, not the elevator, and the musicians carrying large instruments arrive in the rehearsal room slightly winded and sweaty.

In fact, calling the space a rehearsal room is slightly misleading. When Caeli Smith, a viola player, arrived to rehearse, she heard loud, creepy, staticky voices that seemed to emanate from the walls. "I felt like I was in a haunted house," she says. "It was totally not the thing you want to hear before you perform. It was totally not conducive to trying to be quiet and focused." (The noise came from a badly tuned AM radio, which Kageyama had turned to a Spanish-language broadcast of a baseball game, set at high volume, and hidden behind furniture.) By the time Smith was called into the audition room, she recalls, "I was feeling very clammy, not warmed up, and very nervous."

When the musicians entered the audition space, they saw there was no screen. The judges sat at a table in full view, a gigantic difference from what the students had been led to expect. In every case, the judges welcomed the students by mispronouncing their names, or calling them by the wrong names, creating initial confusion. One of the judges noisily munched from a bag of crunchy plantain chips. Another unwrapped candy. Before the musicians had finished getting set up, one judge spoke up: "You can start anytime you like." *Slight pause.* "You can begin now." *Slight pause.* "We're ready." In other words, *hurry up.*

Some students experienced more miscues when they began playing. The pianists noticed that certain keys played strangely. (Kageyama had secretly loaded ping-pong balls inside the piano.) One judge's cell phone went off periodically, and in some instances he took the call. The overall atmosphere, Smith recalls, was extremely unprofessional and distracting.

Of course, that's exactly the point.

This "adversity audition" is the traditional culmination of the Juilliard course. It tests whether the techniques the students have learned help them cope not only in a traditional audition, but even in a worst-case scenario. Sometimes Kageyama asks a judge to drink from a whiskey bottle (filled with iced tea) and appear inebriated. Sometimes he sets up an oscillating fan to blow the musicians' sheet music around while they play. "The judges are instructed to be disrespectful, ornery, rude, and difficult," Kageyama says. By most accounts, they play this role very well.

While the judges do assess the musicians' playing, they're also paying close attention to how well the students cope with the circumstances. Do they let the judges' pressure interfere with their routine before they begin? Do they appear frazzled, distracted, frustrated, or angry? The audition doesn't really count for half the semester's grade, but the judges do crown a winner—one based not just on musicality. Says Kageyama: "We try to pick the one person who seemed to handle everything the best."

This semester's winner is Tomer Gewirtzman, an Israeli-born pianist. When he sat down to play, he realized that Kageyama had outfitted the piano with a chair that sloped forward toward the keyboard, a form of seating that makes it difficult to play well. Even as the judges ordered him to start playing, Gewirtzman stopped, scanned the room, pulled aside the sloped chair, and retrieved a better chair from the other side of the room. "He impressed them, because he took the time—he wasn't rushed at all, and he didn't seem flustered when the ping-pong balls started making noises," Kageyama recalls.

Smith, the viola player, isn't sure how well she'd have dealt with all the discombobulations if she hadn't learned the techniques Kageyama had taught her. Before taking the performance enhancement class, she'd spent the final moments before an audition the way most musicians do: obsessing over the technical challenges of the piece she'd be playing, and frantically replaying the most difficult passages. (Very often, she'd also make repeated trips to the bathroom, as the nerves affected her bladder.) In retrospect, she says, replaying tricky passages is probably the least productive thing you can do right before a performance, because it makes you worry about screwing up, instead of visualizing a good performance. Smith finds it somewhat shocking that while music instructors spend so many hours helping musicians learn how to practice and perform, none of this instruction focuses on developing a smart and effective pre-performance routine.

By the midpoint of this semester, Smith had already incorporated Kageyama's techniques and done a complete makeover of her preshow regimen. Now she doesn't play her viola backstage. Instead, she closes her eyes, breathes, and does the centering exercise her professor taught her. "Once you get good at it, you can do it in about ten seconds," she says. She repeats some simple affirmations, ones that focus not on success, but on doing her best. (An example: "I'm going to feel free to explore all the possibilities of what this music might hold.") If you reread that statement closely, you may notice that she's focusing on the opportunity to play this music, rather than the high stakes or the obligation; in this way, her affirmation is its own form of reappraisal.

Then she consciously tries to unplug from her verbal, rational left brain and plug into her creative and intuitive right brain. "I don't want to have words in my mind. I want to think about what sounds I'm going to make," she says.

It was challenging to do this in the audition room. "The judges kept saying, 'Whenever you're ready, whenever you're ready,'" she recalls, and it was clear they were trying to disrupt her. But she still took a few seconds to herself, and she didn't put her bow to her strings until she was ready. Afterward, she was pleased with her performance. "I did get really nervous. That radio [in the rehearsal space] really freaked me out," she says. "But I was able to deliver what I wanted despite so many distractions," she says.

She attributes that success to using her newfound tools. "I had my routine, and I prepared myself before playing," she says. It's the kind of coolheaded performance to which we all should aspire.

Chapter Two

WHY YOU NEED A PRE-PERFORMANCE RITUAL

CAN ROUTINE AND SUPERSTITION REALLY INCREASE SUCCESS?

For Stephen Colbert, perhaps the most important moment in the long hours leading up to his performance on his Comedy Central show (before he succeeded David Letterman on CBS's *The Late Show*) took place an hour before the curtain, when he'd shave and put on the Brooks Brothers suit chosen by his stylist. "Getting into the character for the show is a long process of fits and starts, because I'm not in character all day. I'm a writer and producer all day," Colbert told *Slate*'s David Plotz in a 2014 podcast. Putting on the suit signified an important moment in that shift, and it was one of a series of steps in Colbert's complicated regimen.

Some of Colbert's preshow routines—like getting his hair and makeup done, and going to the bathroom—are logical things to do before appearing on television. Other behaviors, not so much.

"We have a little bell in the bathroom, which I like ringing for complicated reasons. It's like a hotel bell, DING! I go there and I go, 'All right, have a good show,'" he says. Then Colbert would wait for his producer to say, "Squeeze out some sunshine," as he did every night. Then Colbert touched hands—not a high five, just a touch—with every person working backstage, ending with the teleprompter operator. Then he would grab a box of a particular style of Bic pens, remove one, chew the top, and place the pen back in the box. (Bic no longer manufactures this style of pen, so Colbert's staff used to search stationery stores around the world to buy up any leftover stock.) Then he would slap himself in the face, twice, hard. Then he stared at a particular spot on the theater wall, looked away, then stared at it again. Only then would Colbert take the stage.

Colbert's backstage ritual is unusually elaborate, but nearly every performer does some set of steps to help them reduce anxiety, increase confidence, and get into the right mindset to perform. Midway through the 2002 documentary *Comedian,* there's a scene of Jerry Seinfeld backstage, just before a show. Despite all his success, he's visibly (and surprisingly) nervous. In an interview, I asked Seinfeld about his backstage routine.

"You don't have to get psyched up. The audience will take care of that," Seinfeld told me. "You walk out in front of three thousand people who have paid seventy-five dollars or a hundred dollars, and they're sitting there saying, 'We want to laugh right now.'

You feel that when you walk out on the stage. But every comedian, like every athlete, has a little routine. My routine is to look at my notes until five minutes before the show. . . . When my tour producer says, 'Five minutes,' I put on the jacket, and when the jacket goes on, it's like my body knows, 'OK, now we've got to do our trick.' And then I stand, and I like to just walk back and forth, and then, that's it. That's my little preshow routine. I never vary it, and it seems to just kind of signal everything. It just feels comfortable."

Why does Seinfeld's body respond when he dons his jacket? Why does Colbert feel like he'll perform better if he chews a particular kind of Bic pen before taking the stage? Neither of them really knows why. In a way, it really doesn't matter. These performers *think* their backstage rituals help them perform better. In the strange but virtuous circle that one quickly encounters in the research into ritual and superstition, thinking these things will help probably *does* help them do better, even if no one really understands why.

2.

There are no Venn diagrams in this chapter, but it may be helpful if you construct some in your mind as you think about three interrelated ideas: pre-performance routines, rituals, and superstitious behaviors.

All the things Seinfeld does—and many of the things Colbert

does—before a show fit the definition of a pre-performance routine: a sequence of systematic, task-related thoughts and actions. Over the last thirty years, sports psychologists have conducted dozens of studies into what athletes do before they compete, and the studies generally show that people who use a well-conceived and consistent routine perform better than those who don't.

Some of the studies on pre-performance routines are descriptive. A study of divers, for instance, used stopwatches to measure how long the divers spent on the board before they jumped, and it found divers who engaged in a longer sequence of activities before jumping tended to have better scores.

Some of the studies utilized interventions, in which athletes who didn't use a pre-performance routine were taught to incorporate one, and their before-and-after results were compared against a control group. As in the descriptive studies, the interventions generally showed that athletes who learned to do the same thing every time played their sport better.

"The use of structured routines prior to performances [is] believed to be an extremely important behavioral technique to help performers attain high levels of achievement in sport," writes Stewart Cotterill, a University of Winchester sports psychologist who conducted a metastudy of existing research on pre-performance routines in sports as varied as bowling, water polo, archery, rugby, and darts. The conventional wisdom is that pre-performance routines are particularly helpful for activities such as shooting a free throw (in basketball) or sinking a putt (in golf)—uncontested activities done without a defender's interference, and that rely on mechanics and focus to successfully repeat a rote motion an athlete has practiced thousands of times.

The question is: *Why* do pre-performance routines help?

There's no clear answer. Cotterill cites theories and hypotheses raised by other researchers: that the routines help focus athletes' attention, limit distractions, help to "trigger" movements they've practiced, and help them feel optimistic, energized, and in a confident mental state. These theories all make sense, but there's no way to actually prove what mechanisms are at work. As Cotterill writes: "At a fundamental level it is still not clear what function routines fulfill, what they should consist of or the most effective way to teach them."

Pre-performance routines can be helpful outside of sports, as well. The writer and surgeon Atul Gawande explores this in *The Checklist Manifesto.* Inspired by pilots who've learned to decrease accident rates by using written checklists of activities to be performed both preflight or later, during flight, if an emergency occurs, Gawande describes how he imported pre-performance checklists into his operating rooms. He also documents the improvement in outcomes that stem from systematically following the same set of steps before picking up a scalpel.

Whether you're considering an Olympic sport or a complex surgery, the key words in the definition of a pre-performance routine are "task related." Everything Gawande does prior to operating involves the procedure at hand; everything an Olympic diver does on the board prepares him for the physical task of diving.

Similarly, parts of Stephen Colbert's routine, such as donning makeup and a business suit, are related to the task of hosting a television show.

But what's going on when Colbert rings the hotel bell, chews the pen cap, slaps his face, or stares at the special spot on the wall? They are not task related. They have no apparent connection with performing on TV.

These are more properly thought of as rituals, which are simply things done the same way every time. Note that all pre-performance routines can be called rituals, because they're done the same way every time, but not all rituals can be called routines, since the latter include actions that aren't task related. (Here's where the Venn diagrams can be helpful.)

NBA star LeBron James has a long set of task-related preperformance routines, including warm-up shots, getting taped, and icing his legs, but he also has an additional, complex set of pregame rituals that have evolved over the course of his career. In 2010 they included: forming the numbers 3-3-0 with his fingers after the National Anthem (that's the area code for Akron, his hometown), giving a unique handshake or fist bump to each of his fourteen teammates, asking the referee to hand him the game ball so he can give it a light massage before tip-off, and throwing chalk dust into the air by the scorer's table.

In baseball, perhaps the most ritualistic player of the modern era is Wade Boggs, who played third base (mostly for the Red Sox) in the 1980s and 1990s. He ate chicken before every game, took 117 ground balls during every infield practice, took batting practice at precisely 5:17 P.M. before evening games, and scratched the Hebrew letters spelling the word *chai* into the dirt as he approached home plate to bat—even though he's not Jewish.

Sports rituals are so pervasive that even video games now allow gamers to create their own players who, in addition to having custom-designed physical attributes (including height, skin tone, and hairstyle), can also be assigned specific pregame rituals. On *NBA 2K16*, my sons' favorite Xbox game, available pregame rituals include motions to hype up the crowd (such as chest pounding), making bowling or pitcher's windup motions, or head butting the basket stanchion.

As with pre-performance routines, there's no scientifically convincing explanation for the purpose served by rituals. People find them comforting or soothing. They're thought to relieve anxiety, though it's not clear why. Some believe they give people a sense of control or self-efficacy in an uncertain situation. "A solid routine fosters a well-worn groove for one's mental energies and helps stave off the tyranny of moods," writes Mason Currey, who collected lists of daily practices of great writers and thinkers for his book *Daily Rituals.*

The third type of pregame action is superstition, and the line between ritual and superstition is decidedly blurry. "A routine becomes superstitious when a particular action is given special, magical significance," writes Connecticut College professor Stuart Vyse in *Believing in Magic,* his highly readable overview of research into superstition. Other definitions of superstition highlight the irrationality or lack of logic involved in superstitious behavior. None of the definitions, however, draw a bright line around what constitutes a superstition; much of the parsing seems to lie with intent and depth of belief. Specifically, someone practicing a superstition is more likely to harbor a deep, almost nonsensical belief that the action affects or determines the outcome of a game or event—and that if he fails to perform the superstitious behavior, his performance will suffer as a result. Boggs's idiosyncratic behaviors, for instance, are clearly superstitious, as is neurosurgeon Mark McLaughlin's preference for administering medications in dosages ending with 9s, instead of round numbers.

Superstitions aren't limited to performers themselves. In 2013, Bud Light introduced a series of ads showing beer-drinking football fans watching games on TV while performing rituals— hand gestures, standing barefoot on one foot, twirling remotes, tapping team banners—set to the Stevie Wonder song "Very Superstitious." The tagline: *It's only weird if it doesn't work.*

There are downsides to rituals and superstitions. When taken to an extreme, neurotic, or overly rigid adherence to ritualized behaviors can be a sign of a mental condition such as obsessive-compulsive disorder. Lucky objects can be lost or stolen. Rituals and superstitions can also be preyed on by adversaries as a form of gamesmanship. For instance, opposing teams would sometimes alter their stadium clocks so that they skipped the precise time at which Boggs liked to perform superstitious acts.

At the same time, there's a reasonable body of evidence that doing a routinized set of pre-performance activities—ritualized, superstitious, or not—really can help someone perform better. So as you think about what rituals belong in your own warm-up routine, keep in mind the profound wisdom of Bud Light: *It's only weird if it doesn't work.*

3.

When Lauren Block was an undergraduate at the State University of New York at Albany, she had a pair of white Nike sneakers with a red swoosh. She began wearing them on days she took exams, and she received good grades. They became her lucky exam shoes.

Block's roommate was the same size, and as they got to know each other, they began wearing each other's clothes. When the roommate saw how Block's Nikes seemed to help her earn better grades, she asked permission to wear the lucky exam sneakers, which Block granted. "She did really well on that first exam, so a superstition was born, and she began wearing them to all her exams," Block recalls.

Among college students, exam superstitions are common. In a study, 62 percent reported using a lucky pen or wearing a particular piece of jewelry or clothing to exams; 36 percent touched a lucky object before taking the test; 54 percent tried to sit in the same seat for tests; and 38 percent listened to a particular song just before the test. When I was in college, I had a silver Cross pen that I only used for exams. It had been a gift from a high school teacher, and I recall feeling slightly calmer and more confident when I opened a blue book and let that special pen begin its work.

The origin story of Block's lucky Nikes provides a window into how most superstitions form. Academics use the term "contiguous events," and it describes how humans, upon experiencing a positive event, have a tendency to look at what else was happening at the same time. When they find it, they often see mysterious connections between the unrelated action or object and the positive outcome. They observe correlation but believe there's causation.

The most famous experiment in contiguity as a driver of superstition took place at Harvard in 1948. B. F. Skinner, a psychologist, placed hungry pigeons in a cage outfitted with an automatic feeding device, which delivered pellets of food every fifteen seconds. During the interval between the feedings, the birds tended to wander around in patterns or move their heads in distinctive ways. Skinner noticed that whatever movement or action the birds were doing at the precise moment the food appeared seemed to take on a special significance to them, and they acted it out repeatedly. "Soon the birds were dancing around the chamber as if their movements caused the operation of the feeder," writes Stuart Vyse. The same phenomenon works with the pen you used or the sneakers you wore on the day you crushed that algebra exam: Logically speaking, the pen or the shoes had nothing to do with the positive outcome, but the contiguity makes you believe it did, so suddenly you have a lucky pen or lucky sneakers.

Broadly speaking, superstitions tend to break down into two types: those involving actions (like the birds' head movements), and those involving objects (like sneakers or pens). There is at least some evidence that each type can help boost performance.

In a 2010 study, three researchers from the University of Cologne performed a number of experiments to see how activating superstitions could affect the way subjects performed in tests of motor skills. In one, for instance, fifty-one female students were asked to play a game involving tilting a board so that thirty-six loose balls would each find a place in thirty-six holes in the board. Just before they began, the researcher told some of the girls: "I press the thumbs for you," a German phrase that's roughly equivalent to "I'm crossing my fingers for you." The fingers-crossed group performed the task much faster than the control group.

Lucky objects can help increase performance, too. Lauren

Block, the lucky Nike owner, is now a professor at the City University of New York, and with a colleague, she conducted a series of lab experiments that explored how people performed on various tests when they prepared using study guides that had previously been used by other students. In the experiments, Block listed the earlier exam takers' scores or GPAs, so that the people using the study guide would observe whether the previous user had done well or poorly. This study specifically looked at the influence of "positive contagion," in which a person's essence is thought to rub off on a physical object they've touched. The results: People using a guidebook previously used by a high performer tended to do better than others. The researchers wrote: "This is the first paper to show that specific abilities can transfer through contagion and impact actual performance by changing performance expectations and confidence." They point out that smart managers could utilize this finding as a performance aid at work, by distributing objects (such as pens or computers) previously used by people who are considered unusually smart or creative.

Block cautions that the effect isn't universal. It's more apparent in people she terms "high experiential processors"—that is, people who rely more on faith and intuition, and less on logic.

Indeed, the question of what types of people are more superstitious than others has been explored for years. In general, women are more superstitious than men; people with less formal education and lower intelligence are more superstitious than those with degrees or high IQs; and nonreligious people are more superstitious than the faithful. Certain professions also exhibit higher levels of superstition, including athletes, actors, gamblers, miners, and sailors.

4.

Chad Knaus insists he's not superstitious. He attributes his success as a NASCAR crew chief to a single factor: his work ethic. Outsiders agree with that assessment.

Since 2002, Knaus has led the hundred-person group of mechanics and pit crew who build, support, and repair driver Jimmie Johnson's No. 48 Lowe's Chevrolet, forming one of the most successful racing teams in the history of the sport. In the process, Knaus, forty-five, has earned a reputation for his ninety-hour workweeks. Press clippings call him a workaholic, insanely intense, and single-minded. Before his 2015 marriage to a former Miss Vermont, Knaus burned through a series of girlfriends, with the demise of each relationship publicly attributed to his inability to put aside his work and carve out time for romance.

When you talk to Knaus about how he manages the complex operation that is a modern NASCAR team, he describes workdays that routinely stretch more than twelve hours as he watches many hours of video of prior races, looking for trends and patterns. He'll tell you about his team's statistical operation, and how they're using big data to find the optimal moments for pit stops to refuel and change tires.

So he doesn't believe in superstitions, karma, or good luck? He shrugs. "Not so much," he says. "I'm a believer in the saying 'Luck is what happens when preparation meets opportunity.'"

But if you spend time around the 48 team on the hundred-acre compound it occupies outside Charlotte, North Carolina, you'll spot Knaus engaging in some strange trends and patterns of his own—some of which have no obvious relationship to the business of racing.

There is, for instance, the bonsai tree Knaus keeps in his office. He received his first bonsai as a gift during the 2005 NASCAR season, his fourth year working with Johnson, who at that point had never won the Sprint Cup, NASCAR's season champion. Late that year, with Johnson riding neck and neck in the chase for first place, Knaus became so preoccupied with work that he forgot to water his plant. It died. Around the same time, Johnson finished poorly in a race, knocking him out of contention.

The death of Knaus's bonsai tree and Johnson's failure to win a championship became connected in Knaus's mind as contiguous events.

Soon afterward, Knaus's assistant bought him a replacement bonsai tree. Since he'd drawn this loose mental connection between mistreating his bonsai and watching his race team lose, Knaus began a new set of rituals during Nascar's grueling ten-month season, actions aimed at preventing a reoccurrence of the bad luck bonsai death. Each Thursday afternoon, before boarding the private jet that will fly him to that weekend's race, Knaus spends a few minutes tending to his bonsai. He waters it. He carefully prunes dying leaves. Then, to show respect to the dead foliage, he carries the leaves outside his office and returns them to the earth. "I give it a little love and affection," Knaus says. The ritual is superstitious, but it also serves an inadvertent but useful purpose: Amid an insanely busy and deadline-driven workday, it forces Knaus to take a quiet, reflective pause, to catch his breath before the rush to get to the airfield on time.

Since Knaus got this replacement tree and began taking better care of it, Jimmie Johnson has won seven Nascar championships, including a record five in a row from 2006 to 2010. *It isn't weird if it works.*

Knaus, who was raised in Illinois and began working as a crew member on his father's racing team as a child, says he didn't grow up in an environment focused on rituals or lucky practices. His perspective changed, however, at nineteen, when he moved to North Carolina to begin working full time on NASCAR teams. "When I got to the South, that's when the superstitions came out," Knaus says. For instance, among the racing teams he encountered in Charlotte, there was a unanimous belief that fifty-dollar bills are unlucky. As a result, when office managers go to the bank to retrieve cash and hand out per diem payments to race teams for each week's race, everyone finds it completely normal that the cash is all in tens, twenties, or hundred-dollar bills. Never, ever a fifty.

"Oh yeah, I guess I have another one," Knaus says sheepishly. Early each Thursday morning, before leaving his home for work (and knowing he won't be home until after the race on Sunday night), he hand-winds a grandfather clock he won as a prize in a long-ago NASCAR race. "If I come home on Sunday night and we had a bad race, I look at the clock," he says. "If it's not swinging and it's unwound, I say, 'Well, I guess that's why . . .'"

While Knaus has his individual weekly superstitions, he also participates in the group rituals that have become a part of life on the 48 team. For instance, each February, once the race cars are built, double-checked, and ready to be loaded into trailers to be driven to the season-opening Daytona 500, the team members come together and hand-wax the cars. To put this in perspective, at the time I interviewed him, Knaus lived in a house worth nearly $3 million; he spends much of his workday in meetings and on e-mail and admits he hasn't used a wrench in years. So waxing cars is *way* below his pay grade. But the waxing ritual is an important moment of team bonding. It also illustrates how everyone in the group, no matter what their status or function, is caring for the cars they depend on for their livelihood and success. After the wax is applied, they take a giant Styrofoam replica of a Kobalt hammer—a tool made by their sponsor, Lowe's—and put it on the hood of the car as it's loaded up into the trailer. "It signifies that the car is done, and it's ready to go to the racetrack," says Knaus.

The rituals don't end when the race does. When Johnson or one of the other three drivers from Hendrick Motorsports wins a race on Sunday, the following morning a large, wheeled replica of the Liberty Bell is pushed around the company's campus. Each employee takes a turn ringing it to celebrate the victory.

Johnson, who spends Sunday afternoons strapped into the driver's seat, doesn't overthink his team's lucky rituals. "We like to joke that we're not sure we're superstitious, but we like to cover our bases just in case," Johnson told me a few days after winning a big race. For instance, Johnson admits to being continually on the lookout for heads-up pennies on the ground, which he likes to retrieve and glue to the dashboard of his racecar.

Johnson says, "At different times in my career I have felt that superstitions may have helped. It's all just a mindset. The power of our minds and brains is massive, and modern medicine is just starting to recognize the effects of positive attitude."

5.

Knaus's set of prerace activities gives rise to an important question. Some prerace rituals, like trimming the bonsai tree, he does alone. It's a solo, one-person ritual. Other activities—waxing the car, ringing the bell—are done as part of a group.

So for people participating in a group performance, are individual rituals or group rituals more effective?

A few years ago, Harvard Business School professor Michael Norton and some colleagues tried to answer that question. They began by gathering 221 people and giving them a strange assignment. They had to form groups of 2 to 4 people and run around the campus, taking group selfies in front of specific locations. They were given exactly forty-five minutes, with points deducted from their score for every minute they were late returning to the meeting point. The group that photographed themselves in the most spots would win a cash prize.

Before this selfie scavenger hunt began, however, there was one important thing that some of the groups had to do. They were instructed to form a circle and perform a series of rhythmic claps and foot stomps, followed by putting their hands into middle and shouting "Let's go"—a routine they performed three times, getting a little faster each time.

The other groups didn't do a ritual. Instead, they were instructed to spend a few minutes reading an article in silence.

When the scavenger hunt was finished, the results showed the groups that had executed the prehunt ritual performed better in several ways. They successfully photographed themselves at more locations, on average. They were less than half as likely to have missed the forty-five-minute deadline. In a posthunt survey, the groups that had done the clapping ritual reported liking each other more than the groups that had read in silence.

In other experiments, Norton and his colleagues had hundreds of people do group creativity tasks, such as brainstorming how many uses they could devise for an object. In these tests, everyone had to do a strange ritual involving rolling dice and waving arms in patterns. Some people did the ritual solo, sitting alone in a cubicle; others did it as a group. The results showed that doing the dice-and-wave routine in a group increased the team's creativity and led members to like each other more. Anecdotally, the researchers also noticed that the ritual groups were more likely to do things that weren't an assigned part of the experiment, such as coming up with team names, or arranging a group lunch afterward.

Norton, who earned a doctorate in psychology at Princeton and is now a professor in Harvard's marketing department, first became interested in rituals after reading Harvard president Drew Faust's 2008 book, *This Republic of Suffering: Death and the American Civil War*. The book chronicled how the nation dealt with losing 2 percent of its population—more than six hundred thousand men—on battlefields in just four years. The war changed the way people talked and thought about death, as well as how they grieved.

"One of the things that really struck me about how people

dealt with death was the rituals, in particular, the clothing rituals in the South," Norton says. Under the system that evolved, mourners would wear black clothing for a certain period of time, and then gray clothing, and then a small bit of lavender clothing. The clothing progression seemed to serve multiple purposes. It helped give the mourners a road map and a timetable for navigating their grief, and it helped give those in contact with the mourners a visual reminder of precisely where the grief-stricken individual was in their journey beyond their loved one's death.

The system seems to make sense, but as a student of psychology, Norton began asking himself precisely what emotional purpose it served. Do rituals really work to make people feel better? If so, how and why? Do they only affect our emotions, or, by affecting our emotions, can they affect how we perform tasks? Norton poured through existing literature on rituals, much of it done by anthropologists. It was vividly descriptive—lots of the studies involved primitive tribal groups—but there was nothing experimental and nothing that sought to show or understand cause and effect. Over the next few years, he and some colleagues aimed to fill that void.

In addition to the paper on group rituals, Norton has coauthored three other studies on rituals. One studied how rituals affect consumption, and required subjects to engage in various actions—elaborate unwrapping, knocking on desks, deep breaths, closing eyes—before eating chocolate, carrots, and lemonade. A second study examined how rituals affect how people feel about relationships that ended, deaths, or financial losses. The studies showed that rituals increase people's consumption experience by increasing their involvement. (This is why restaurants engage in fussy bottle-opening and tasting regimens when serving wine.) They also found that rituals help people feel better after losses, even if they claim not to be big believers in rituals.

Norton also partnered with Alison Wood Brooks, the Harvard colleague whose reappraisal research was featured in Chapter One, to study how rituals affect pre-performance anxiety. In a reprise of the methodology used in Brooks's dissertation, they had subjects sing "Don't Stop Believin'" using Wii karaoke in front of a researcher. However, beforehand, half the subjects were told to perform a specific ritual. (The instructions: "Draw a picture of how you are feeling right now. Sprinkle salt on your drawing. Count up to five out loud. Crinkle up your paper. Throw your paper in the trash.") The singers who completed the ritual sang significantly better and reported feeling less anxiety when singing. In follow-up experiments, they found that singers who performed a ritual exhibited fewer physical signs of anxiety (measured by heart rate); that rituals also helped people do better on a math test; and that telling the subjects they were doing a "ritual" led to better performance than if they did the exact same actions but called them "random gestures."

Norton explains: "There seems to be something about rituals

that in this context reduces anxiety and helps you do a little bit better."

The experiments offer proof that rituals can cause better performances, but they don't explain why. When Norton reflects on the research, particularly the study involving anxiety, he focuses on the distraction element of the ritual. "Perhaps rituals work not because they're magically amazing, but they're just better than what we usually do," Norton says. This makes special sense if what we'd ordinarily do is worry—a pretty common activity before a big performance.

6.

According to union rules, an actor in a Broadway production cannot be required to arrive at the theater more than thirty minutes before a performance. Nevertheless, Belfast-born actress Laura Donnelly likes to show up several hours before the curtain. She needs time to shake off the bustle and noise of the Manhattan streets. She eats a relaxed takeout dinner in the theater, then takes off her shoes and, clad in a tracksuit, does yoga. She runs and jumps around backstage, limbering her muscles. Next is a series of vocal exercises, before she goes to her dressing room to don makeup and costume and meditate on the character she'll be playing that night.

"I warm up the same way before any play. I have my set

routine," says Donnelly, who is best known for her role in the TV series *Outlander* and in movies such as *The Program*. The regimen hasn't varied much since she learned it in drama school years ago.

But in the fall of 2014, when Donnelly starred alongside Hugh Jackman in the Broadway show *The River,* Donnelly was forced to put aside her traditional pre-performance routine and do something else instead.

Before each matinee and evening performance, the show's director asked the show's three actors, the stage manager, and one or two other key backstage personnel to form a circle in the theater's lobby. Each night, the group would agree on a new category. Sometimes it involved something from the play; more often, it was something random, such as a type of tree, or a sexual position, or a cartoon character who is blue. Then one of the actors would take an American football, shout an example that fit the category (say, *Papa Smurf!*), and toss the football to the person directly across the circle, who'd then shout her word (*Superman!*), and toss the football onward. After the entire group had caught and thrown the football a few times, they'd choose a second category, and, with the football still making its rounds, start shouting a second set of words and tossing a tennis ball to each other. Often the circle would disintegrate as the cast moved around the lobby, the tosses growing longer, creating pressure to locate the intended target. "It got sillier and sillier. That was the charm of the game," Donnelly says. "We'd usually end up falling down and laughing."

After ten minutes or so of tossing balls, the group would re-form the circle and begin rhythmically clapping and telling a sequential story, with each person contributing two syllables and the next person picking up the semicoherent storyline.

When the show's director first told Donnelly that he wanted her to incorporate the ball tossing into her preshow routine—supplanting some of her usual solo drills—she recalls being slightly miffed. "It felt like I was being taken out of my ability to control how I warm up, and I guess I felt a little out of my comfort zone," she says. Over time, her view shifted. "I began to realize that this was much more beneficial than my own personal warm-up," she says. Donnelly recalls many other theatrical productions, with actors warming up individually, in which she'd find herself onstage reciting dialogue with a cast member to whom she hadn't even had time to say "hello" before the curtain rose. "[The group ritual] was a really great way of reconnecting. It gave us such a sense of being one company, and a real camaraderie, that was really useful," Donnelly says. "It's something I'd be very keen to do with any company in the future."

Ian Rickson, the show's director, has never heard of Mike Norton nor his Harvard research, but after more than two decades of leading productions in the theaters of London and New York, he knows in his bones that group rituals make a big difference.

"Actors are like athletes, and they need the same rigor and

care that Usain Bolt might take before running one hundred meters. They need their own runway into a performance," he says. "In my experience the really committed and interesting actors are really quite thorough about what their warm-up is before a performance." And while many actors are inclined to engage in individual pre-performance routines, Rickson often encourages them to create new rituals that take place in groups. "Different plays demand different runways, and I like to customize it to the show and the particular actors," he says.

Like Donnelly, some actors are resistant at first. Lately yoga and customized music playlists on iPhones have become the prevailing backstage norm. "The etiquette is that the hour before the performance is the actor's time. An actor is allowed to say 'I want to do my own thing,'" Rickson says. "But I quite like to be involved, and I'm keen on creating some sort of ritual that is connective, that creates trust among people."

While Rickson is known for investing unusual energy and creativity to create group-oriented preshow routines, backstage rituals are a part of life on Broadway. Some of them are purely superstitious and focused on creating or preserving good luck. Cast and crew know never to whistle anywhere near the stage or to mention the play *Macbeth* (always refer to it vaguely as "the Scottish play"); both actions are thought to bring bad luck.

The most elaborate preshow ritual, dating from the 1950s, involves a garment called the Gypsy Robe. On the opening night of a new Broadway musical, the entire cast and crew assemble onstage, and a veteran dancer from the most recent musical to open arrives with a pieced together, quiltlike robe, to which every Broadway musical has sewn its own small piece of fabric. After recounting the history of the robe, the representative from the prior Broadway play places it on the shoulders of the most senior chorus member of tonight's show. While wearing the robe, the new gypsy circles the cast counterclockwise three times, touching each person on each pass. Then, after the assemblage breaks up, the gypsy takes the robe to each performer's dressing room for a brief visit.

Other rituals are a function of the grueling and sometimes monotonous grind of the eight-times-a-week performing schedule. "Certainly on long-running Broadway shows, the rituals are a curb-to-curb experience," says Michael Passaro, who's worked as a stage manager for more than thirty years. "Walking through the stage door, picking up their dressing room key, signing in at the call board, and getting into the routine, anything they can do to help focus them prior to the show, the better they're going to be," he says.

During the 2013 production of Nora Ephron's *Lucky Guy*, starring Tom Hanks in his Broadway debut, Hanks led the cast in what the *New York Times* described as a "small riot" a half hour before each show. The cast played kazoos, harmonicas, and duck whistles as a helium balloon was released; when it hit the skylight, the noise instantly stopped. As curtain time approached, the cast acted out silly walks and recited vulgar chants together. At the same time each night, Hanks would blast the Linda Ronstadt song "You're No Good." Hanks told the newspaper, "It's the next one of the 57 things that have to happen before every show."

Reflecting back on the warm-up routine he created for *The River*, Rickson asks the key question when it comes to pre-performance rituals: "Do these things make a difference?" He answers: "From a director's point of view, they do. Like great sports players or great public speakers, when you engage the footballer or the poet or the musician, or in this case the actors, in a dynamic way of absolutely being in the present and connected to their fellow players, something really special happens."

Critics agreed. Reviewing *The River*, the *New York Times*'s Ben Brantley said Jackman "ascends with assurance to a new level as a stage actor," that Rickson directs "with care and polish," and that the play "is guaranteed to hold your attention."

7.

One of my favorite research studies about superstition was done by a team led by Sally Linkenauger. The researchers assembled forty-one right-handed golfers of equal ability who were asked to attempt ten putts from a distance of two meters on an artificial green. As in most of the experiments described in this chapter, the golfers were divided into two groups. As the researcher handed over the expensive putter each would use to attempt the shots, half the subjects were told that the club had previously been owned by Ben Curtis, a well-known PGA player, while the others weren't told anything about the club's provenance. (The researchers were lying—Curtis never owned the club.) Before putting, each golfer was asked to estimate the size of the golf hole by drawing it, and then attempt the ten putts.

The results showed that the golfers who thought they were using a PGA player's club estimated the hole was 9 percent larger (suggesting the shot looked easier), and they sank 32 percent more putts than the control group.

After reading the study, I interviewed Linkenauger for a section of *Harvard Business Review* called "Defend Your Research," in which we conduct slightly skeptical Q&As with academics whose research seems to defy common sense. The headline on the piece read: "YOU'LL GOLF BETTER IF YOU THINK TIGER HAS USED YOUR CLUBS."

In the interview, Linkenauger attributed the results to "positive contagion." "This is part of the reason people value autographs. The fact that a famous person has touched and signed the paper makes it feel very intimate, as if the person has given you a piece of themselves," she said. It's old news that celebrity artifacts are valuable, but this was the first study to suggest that a celebrity's essence on a tool might actually help enhance someone's performance.

I asked a simple follow-up question: "If I wrote an article using Malcolm Gladwell's laptop, would it be perceptibly better?"

Linkenauger says her team had debated similar questions, such as whether using a pen owned by Einstein might help someone score better on a math exam. Their research suggested that it might, perhaps because the famous person's tool helps prime a person to emulate the celebrated person's success. She concluded, "If it makes you more confident and motivated, it will help you perform better."

As I geared up to write this book, I kept returning to this question: Would it turn out better if I wrote it on Malcolm Gladwell's laptop?

Years ago, before he became a literary celebrity, Gladwell and I had worked as reporters at different publications located in the same Manhattan office tower. We'd met a few times: His office had a Bloomberg terminal and mine didn't, so I used to drop by to use it.

So I e-mailed Gladwell, reintroduced myself, and made an offer: If I sent him a brand-new keyboard, would he write on it for three months and then return to me? I explained that I hoped to write my book on a keyboard he'd used, to test if positive contagion really makes a difference.

He replied a few hours later: "Ha. That's hilarious." He specified that he'd need a Mac keyboard, and gave me his address.

The next day I shipped him a new white Apple keyboard,

along with some Sharpies and a note encouraging him to sign, decorate, or otherwise mark the keyboard to indicate he'd used it. A couple of months later, I checked in. "Yes! I've been using it!" he replied. "Just give me a reminder when you need it back." I told him to keep it another month or so. A month later, eager to start writing, I asked him to ship it back. No reply. I asked again. No reply. And again.

Days passed. I began to worry that Gladwell had been scamming me. Maybe he just wanted a free keyboard, and had never really planned on returning it.

A week later, I see his name in my in-box. "So sorry I haven't been in touch! I've been traveling for three weeks and went on e-mail hiatus. I'm back on Tuesday and will send the keyboard asap. I have been using it—and hope I have transferred some magic powers!"

The keyboard arrived a few days later. Gladwell hadn't signed or marked it with the Sharpies, so aside from the e-mail trail, there's no evidence he'd actually used it. One colleague who watched me open the package offered unhelpful commentary: "You *think* he was writing his next book on it, but what if he just used it for stupid things like Facebook?"

Over the coming months, I carried the Apple keyboard around, using it only when working on this book. To be honest, it was a pain. At work I ordinarily use a special ergonomic keyboard to protect against repetitive stress injuries; by comparison,

Gladwell's standard keyboard felt unfamiliar and uncomfortable. All the transport took its toll: After just a few months, one of the keys fell off.

Still, I did get a small thrill knowing my fingers were striking the same keys as the fingers that had written *Outliers* and *The Tipping Point.* Did it increase my confidence by some small percentage? Yes! The book certainly didn't write itself, and to preempt the too-easy line before any critic uses it: Yes, I know, I'm definitely no Malcolm Gladwell.

But as I sat there typing away on Gladwell's keyboard, I couldn't help but think of the moments when he must have struggled to find the right words but persevered. Decades after I lost my lucky Cross exam pen, I'm happy to have a lucky keyboard to rely on for a little boost. It may be a little weird, but for me, it works.

Chapter Three

DON'T JUST WIN ONE FOR THE GIPPER

IS AN EMOTIONAL PEP TALK ALWAYS MOST EFFECTIVE?

I n 2005, a friend invited Erica Galos Alioto to the launch party for an Internet start-up called Yelp. She needed a night out. A graduate of Berkeley Law, Alioto worked at a large corporate law firm, and it was mind-numbing. "You can make it through the day," she'd tell herself every morning, psyching herself up for a job she couldn't stand.

Yelp had just launched a Web site where consumers could post reviews of businesses. Alioto loved the party, and afterward she began writing Yelp reviews herself. She wrote so many she soon began earning invites to parties for "elite" reviewers. The more she used Yelp, the more she liked it.

In late 2005 she called Yelp and asked if they needed legal help. The company wasn't yet big enough to need an in-house lawyer, but they did need a salesperson. Was she interested?

Alioto became one of Yelp's first fifteen employees.

She learned to sell by trial and error, calling up local businesses and urging them to pay for an ad on the Web site. Closing sales was a challenge, since almost no one she called had ever heard of Yelp.

But Alioto, who is talkative and energetic, was good at her new job. Soon she was promoted to sales manager. Then she was promoted again. And again.

Nearly ten years later, on the last Friday of August, Alioto awoke in a Manhattan hotel room. She put on a pair of impossibly shiny, sequined, look-at-me gold pants: a lucky outfit she only wears on LDOM, Yelp's term for "Last Day of the Month." After breakfast, she donned headphones, cranked up the song "Chop Suey!" by the band System of a Down, and headed to Yelp's New York office.

Alioto, thirty-nine, is Yelp's senior vice president for local sales. Just before 9 A.M., she stands at the front of the auditorium. Looking on are 650 sales reps, mostly in their twenties, dressed in summer casual. They are just a portion of the 1,750 reps who report to Alioto, whose unit is responsible for more than 80 percent of Yelp's new revenue.

Taking the microphone, her goal is simple: to get these salespeople fired up to sell as many ads as possible today, before the accountants close the books on this month.

Giving an energizing, motivating, confidence-building pep

talk is a basic duty of a sales executive, one dramatized in movies like *Glengarry Glen Ross* and *The Wolf of Wall Street*. It's a task Alioto has worked hard to perfect.

"Wow, let me just say I'm impressed. I'm impressed first of all how big this group has gotten," she begins. "I was here just a few months ago and it seems like you guys are multiplying at a crazy pace." In fact, this office is adding ninety new salespeople every month.

She extols the group for being the top-producing sales office at Yelp so far in August. She namechecks the office's big producers.

She speaks for twenty minutes. The heart of the talk is about setting specific goals for the day, and her explication of the formula she lays out: "Success Equals Mentality plus Attitude plus Talent." Everyone in the room has the talent to succeed, she says. They couldn't have made it through Yelp's hiring gauntlet if they didn't. So she suggests ways for them to shift into the right mentality and attitude. She tells stories. She asks questions. She instructs the audience to write down their goals for the day on a Post-it, and stick it on their computer.

Then her volume rises as she urges the group to get energized for LDOM, a day when Yelpers typically close two to four times as many sales as they do on ordinary days.

"LDOM is not about the day of the month. It's how we approach that day," she says. "There's something about that day that makes us come in with a ridiculous amount of grit and determination—the ability to make the unthinkable happen. . . . All those people who've been telling us no all month long, we're going to turn them around and get a yes."

Loud clapping.

"This office is currently $1.5 million away from target this month. . . . Everything you do today, every action you take to make that successful outcome, every time you pitch, every business owner you talk to, every time you encourage a teammate to be better, every time you win the heart and mind of a business owner, it's helping not only you, but it's helping your team, it's helping your office, it's helping the organization. It helps Yelp get to where it wants to be.

"We have an action plan here. All we need to do is go execute today." She pauses. "Are you going to execute?" There's moderate applause. She asks again, with a slightly annoyed edge: *"Are we going to execute?"* Big applause.

The reps file back to their phones. Today each will call and ask seventy business owners to buy Yelp ads. Each time they succeed, they run to the front of the room and hit a big gong, as coworkers cheer.

2.

Most of the chapters in this book are about psyching yourself up. But there comes a moment in life when it's not about us anymore: It's about the people we're leading. We can't do it for them. We can teach, encourage, prod, and cajole, but the outcome is in their hands. In the final few moments, all we can offer is a pep talk.

There is a lot of mythology around pep talks. They have been celebrated for decades in sports films and war movies. NFL and NBA coaches' pregame speeches are now routinely broadcast live on TV. Executives must deliver rousing remarks at every product launch or at the end of a quarter.

No one is really taught to give these talks. We learn them mostly by mimicry and intuition. Some people are naturally good at them, but many aren't.

That's especially true in Silicon Valley, where many of the people leading companies are highly introverted young men who've spent most of their lives with their faces buried in computer screens.

So for many years, uncharismatic tech executives have tried to solve that problem by placing a call to Coach Bill Campbell.

Campbell was born and raised in Homestead, Pennsylvania, an old steel town. While playing high school football, Campbell remembers his coach diverting the team bus on their way to a game against their archrival, Mount Lebanon High School. Instead of going directly to the field, the bus toured the adjoining neighborhood of ritzy homes. "You see those Cadillacs?" the coach asked. "Your fathers make the steel that goes into those Cadillacs.

Are you going to let those candy-asses beat you?" Campbell recalls walking off the bus so energized that he wanted to strangle somebody. "That was the kind of motivation they used—we were the poor kids from the steelworks, they were the rich kids on the hill, and I'll be damned if we were going to get beat," Campbell says. "Of all the pep talks I've had in my whole life, I'll never forget him saying that."

After high school, Campbell attended Columbia, where he captained the football team. After graduating, he became a football coach, eventually coaching Columbia's team from 1974 to 1979. From there, Campbell moved into a job in advertising and eventually became vice president of sales at Apple, just as it was about to launch the Macintosh computer.

Campbell had no technical or computer skills, but Apple already had plenty of people who did. Instead, he excelled at skills befitting a former football coach: He could identify and nurture talent, build teams, and get everyone to do their best work. Campbell went on to senior jobs at several companies, including Intuit, where he served as CEO. During more than thirty years in Silicon Valley, Campbell—whom everyone called Coach—became especially famous for mentoring young technology wunderkinds with limited people skills. A memorable *Fortune* profile called him "a profane cosmic mash-up of Oprah, Yoda, and Joe Paterno," who has a "preternatural ability to fire people up about their work." (Another nickname: "The Nerd Whisperer.") Campbell became exceptionally close to Steve Jobs, whom he counseled during long walks around their Palo Alto neighborhood.

During his career, Campbell rarely gave on-the-record interviews to reporters, and my conversation with him, not long before his death at age seventy-five in early 2016, was likely the final interview of his life. In our conversation, he described how he'd recently worked with a tech CEO who's not a particularly motivational speaker. The company was going through a period of malaise and infighting. Campbell tried to coach him for a crucial companywide speech. At one point, the CEO gave up and asked Campbell to deliver the talk for him. "No—you're the CEO, and they want to hear from you, from your f—— lips," Campbell said.

He told the young CEO to talk about why he started the company and to explain what he needs them to do, and why. "What they want is to hear your heartbeat—they want you to say what you believe in. They want to believe it's you talking, that you didn't read it from a f—— script. That it's you. You don't have to holler it—*just say it.*"

Campbell watched as the CEO stood in the cafeteria on a Friday afternoon. "He was so unbelievably good," Campbell recalls. "He said it in his words, from the heart. He needed to take a strong stand: 'This is who we are, and this is how we'll succeed.'" The employees responded well, Campbell recalled, and the speech became an important moment in the company's turnaround.

Score another victory for the Nerd Whisperer.

3.

Five minutes into the film *Rudy,* about an undersized walk-on to the Notre Dame football team, a young boy stands in his bedroom as a phonograph plays. Through the crackle of the vinyl recording comes the voice of Knute Rockne, the Notre Dame football coach from the 1920s, recreating one of his pregame speeches: *"And we're going to go inside them, we're going to go outside them. Inside them. Outside them . . . Don't forget men, today's the day we're going to win. Fight! Fight! Fight!"* As the coach yells, a young Rudy Ruettiger yells along, having memorized the words—the first sign of his intense relationship with Notre Dame football.

When Angelo Pizzo was around ten, someone gave him a record containing this Rockne speech. Pizzo memorized the words, just like Rudy. Pizzo recalls that when he was growing up in Indiana in the 1950s, Rockne, who died in a 1931 plane crash, was still revered. "The Knute Rockne speech—it became part of our media culture and our sports culture," he says.

Angelo Pizzo is the screenwriter behind *Rudy,* as well as *Hoosiers* and some other sports movies. When he wrote the scene in which a young Rudy memorizes Rockne's words, he was really describing himself. And over the last thirty years, Pizzo's work has shaped the popular understanding of what coaches should say in those critical pregame moments.

"At this point I've written so many scenes of locker-room

speeches," Pizzo says wearily, admitting that he finds it hard to come up with new lines for coaches to say before the game. Pizzo, sixty-one, is sitting in his expansive study, which contains a massive triangular desk constructed from the hardwood floor taken from the University of Indiana basketball arena, which is a few miles north of his home in Bloomington, Indiana. "I don't want to repeat myself, and there are only so many moves you can make in a locker room."

The idea that a coach's pregame speech can have an outsized effect on the players' performance didn't originate with Rockne. Biographer Ray Robinson notes that the early twentieth century, baseball managers John McGraw and Connie Mack each viewed the pregame speech as a powerful tool. Nor did the skill come naturally: As a young man, Rockne stammered badly, and it was only after diligent work with an elocution coach that he developed a level of comfort speaking in front of his players.

Once he did, however, he became known as a master of the form. Often his pregame speeches relied on theatrical tactics. Sometimes, Robinson writes, Rockne would break down in tears; in at least one instance, in a stadium with thin walls, Rockne remained silent and urged his players to eavesdrop on the opposing coach's pep talk, which denigrated the Irish and served to fire them up.

Rockne is best remembered for his 1928 speech in a game against Army. Down 6-0 at halftime, Rockne told his players about the deathbed scene, eight years earlier, when Irish football standout George Gipp succumbed to pneumonia. "I've got to go, Rock," Rockne recalled Gipp telling him. "It's all right. I'm not afraid. Sometimes when things are going wrong, when the breaks are beating the boys, tell them to go out and win one for the Gipper. I don't know where I'll be then, Rock, but I'll know about it, and I'll be happy."

The Irish rallied to win the game, 12-6, and the "Win one for the Gipper" speech became celebrated by journalists and filmmakers. (Ronald Reagan played Gipp in the 1940 film *Knute Rockne, All American*.) But the veracity of the tale has long been debated. It's not clear Rockne was present during Gipp's final hours, and during his life Gipp was never been known as "the Gipper." Others question the timing. "The fact that Rockne never revealed a syllable of this remarkable valedictory until eight years later . . . must cast some doubt about its authenticity," writes Robinson.

Nonetheless, the legend of Rockne's pregame oratory turned the task of delivering inspirational pep talks into a job requirement for coaches.

As a filmmaker, Angelo Pizzo's work would build on it. After attending the film school at the University of Southern California, in 1976 he took a studio job. "I made my oats going into a script, taking copious notes, breaking it down, analyzing it, and observing all the details to make it better," he says. "I read probably a thousand screenplays before I wrote one."

When he did, at age thirty-one, he depicted a small-town Indiana basketball team's unlikely run to the state championship. The project bounced around Hollywood; eventually, Gene Hackman signed on and a studio green-lit the film; Dennis Hopper and Barbara Hershey came aboard in supporting roles. David Anspaugh, Pizzo's fraternity brother, directed and Pizzo produced. They filmed *Hoosiers* over forty days in sleepy Indiana towns. As Gayle L. Johnson recounts in *The Making of Hoosiers,* they hired mostly nonactors to play the basketball players because they didn't think they could teach actors to dribble and shoot. The film was nominated for two Academy Awards, but Pizzo blew off the Oscars to watch Indiana play for the NCAA basketball championship on television.

More than three decades later, the film enjoys an astonishing afterlife. When I ask leaders about pep talks, people in all walks of life—not just sports coaches, but military officers and C-suite executives—cite *Hoosiers* as a seminal influence. Bill Campbell told me he rewatched the film at least once a year.

But when you watch closely and analyze the locker-room speeches in *Hoosiers,* you'll start to see that they're all not about motivation, rah-rah, and energy.

In the movie, Hackman's character, Coach Norman Dale, gives three distinct pregame speeches, and each is unique.

The first, twenty-five minutes into the film, takes place in a dingy basement locker room before the team's first game. It focuses entirely on strategy: Pass the ball four times before every shot, Hackman nervously tells the team before the chaplain leads them in prayer. He says nothing that's aimed at firing them up.

The second takes place during the semifinals of the state championship tournament. Instead of firing the team up, it urges them to put aside the emotions they may be feeling and to remember the basic basketball strategies that brought them this far. "Forget about the crowd, the size of the school, their fancy uniforms, and remember what got you here," Dale says. "Focus on the fundamentals we've gone over time and time again. And most important, don't get caught up in thinking about winning or losing this game. If you put your effort and concentration into playing to your potential, to being the best you can be, I don't care what the scoreboard says at the end of the game. We're going to be winners. Okay?"

This speech echoes research by Stanford psychologist Carol Dweck, who's found that focusing on inputs (such as effort) instead of outputs (such as winning or losing) puts people into a "growth mindset" that helps them perform better and improve over time.

Coach Dale's third speech takes place on the bench with nineteen seconds remaining in the championship game. The coach outlines a play in which star player Jimmy Chitwood is used as a decoy, and another player takes the final shot. The players silently protest, so the Coach relents, instructing Jimmy to shoot the game winner. The message is clear: The coach is no longer in charge because the team has earned the ability to motivate and manage itself.

Sitting in his study, Pizzo describes the sequence of Hoosiers pep talks this way: "It's a classic Aristotelian three-act structure. Shakespeare used it. There's a protagonist, at a critical point in the last act, who sees something he was blind to. 'I once was blind but now I see.' . . . I was looking for a place where Dale could let go and not be controlling. That came in that final scene. He realized they're a team."

Viewers may come away from the pep talks in *Hoosiers* feeling energized. Indeed, Michael Phelps watched the movie the evening before his Olympics competitions. But listen closely. They're not just about winning one for the Gipper. Yes, they appeal to the player's emotions, but they also focus on the game plan and the specifics of precisely what the team needs to do to win the game.

Maybe Coach Bill Campbell was only half right. Speaking from the heart is great, but conveying actual information and strategy is important, too.

4.

Centuries before the invention of basketball, and long before millennials toiled to sell online advertising to pizza parlors, leaders gave pep talks to soldiers in the moments before battle.

In 1991, Keith Yellin was a doctoral student at the University of Wisconsin who was working on a dissertation about "battle exhortation"—his phrase for precombat pep talks. Like all writers, Yellin was procrastinating. But in the annals of procrastination, few have gone so far as Yellin.

While he was doing his research, the first Gulf War broke out. Yellin began watching CNN's coverage of the war. He began to think his dissertation would benefit from some firsthand experience. He also felt stirrings of patriotism. So he put his dissertation on hold and enlisted in the U.S. Marine Corps.

By the time Yellin completed Officer Candidates School, the Gulf War was long over. Yellin eventually attained the rank of captain, but he didn't see many pep talks during his service. "There's a striking difference between the way you hear about battle exhortation being delivered in histories and what actually happens on the modern battlefield," he says. "Ancient battles, right up to the American Revolution, were often very formal, so two armies would draw up in a line, within eyeshot of one another, providing a perfect opportunity for the senior commander to turn to the troops just before the commencement of hostilities and say 'Okay, this is it, boys.' You might have five minutes or even fifty minutes to get your troops pumped up. But as warfare has evolved, it's become huge, it's become sneaky, and it's become very fast. . . . In my experience in the Marines, the only battle exhortation you'd get was some memo published by the commanding general after hostilities had started."

After Yellin's discharge, he completed his dissertation, called *Battle Exhortation: The Rhetoric of Combat Leadership.* In it, he analyzed precombat speeches by the ancient Greeks and Romans and in Shakespeare's plays. He points to Henry V's "Once more unto the breach" oratory, which is, along with George Patton's speeches to the Third Army before D-Day, considered the finest example of the genre.

He writes that changes in the speed and formality of battle are just one reason precombat pep talks seem to be on the decline. Another important factor: Today's armies are professionalized, made up mostly of career soldiers who voluntarily enlisted. That's in contrast with World War II, which was fought largely by very young "citizen-soldiers," some of whom were drafted. In general, younger, less experienced people need more extrinsic (or outside) motivation (and can benefit more from a rah-rah pep talk, at least at first), while self-selected people who've experienced combat repeatedly are thought to be more intrinsically or self-motivated. They need less energizing and more information.

Perhaps the most useful piece of Yellin's research is a chart in which he lists twenty-three "Common topics" that commanders use in the prebattle speeches he studied. Some of them are very focused on warfare and not particularly useful to someone trying to rev up a sales force. (Themes like "Death is glorious" and "Defend your country" probably won't help motivate your sales team.) But some are useful to a leader giving a pep talk in any context.

The "Unit is ready" talks about how prepared the team is for the fight. "Reputation" focuses on how one's behavior will affect one's future standing. "Reward" highlights the spoils and commendations of victory. "Force comparison" allows the leader to elucidate his team's strengths versus the other team's weaknesses.

Twenty-three variables is a lot to keep track of, so it's not surprising that an on-the-ground commander may find a simpler formula.

Stanley McChrystal is a thirty-eight-year Army veteran and retired four-star general. He ran the U.S. Joint Special Operations Command from 2003 until 2008, and later commanded all forces in Afghanistan. (He retired in 2010, following intemperate comments about Obama administration officials published in a *Rolling Stone* article.) While leading JSOC, McChrystal commanded SEALs, Rangers, and Delta Force operators during some of the fiercest periods of fighting in the war on terror, giving him tons of experience in rallying troops facing a dangerous situation.

But when it comes to pep talks, his view echoes Yellin's. Modern warfare has rendered the purely emotional pep talk far less important than in the past.

"If you went out with Delta Force or the Rangers or the SEALS in this last war, we were fighting every night," McChrystal told me. "Sometimes, as the intelligence matured, they might do three raids a night, one after another. It was a different environment. It wasn't a case of getting yourself up for the big game, like it was the Super Bowl, because you're playing every night. This stuff is happening so fast, they're all business. There wasn't much room for that sort of psyching up. It was assumed that level of motivation was there."

That last sentence is worth repeating: *It was assumed that level of motivation was there.* That's why most Special Forces precombat discussion is strategic, focusing on the plan for the mission.

McChrystal offers some caveats. Earlier in his career, while leading a younger group of greener soldiers, he would sometimes offer final words that focused more on emotion and motivation instead of strategy. "The last thirty minutes or so, it's more about building the confidence and the commitment to each other," he says. But for the most part, instead of talking from his heart about winning one for the Gipper, McChrystal's pep talks focused more on the specifics of the task at hand, what a football coach would call the Xs and Os, or a CEO would call the company's strategy.

When McChrystal gives these talks, he tends to follow a simple, easy to replicate five-part formula: *Here's what I'm asking you to do. Here's why it's important. Here's why I know you can do it. Think about what you've done together before. Now let's go and do it.*

There's motivation in that formula, but the emphasis is on the first part, what exactly the soldiers should do.

For evidence that this strategy-focused methodology has become the dominant approach to military pep talks, it's worth examining the oratory just prior to one of the most celebrated American military missions of the last fifty years: Operation Neptune Spear, in which twenty-three Navy SEALs flew into Pakistan and killed Osama bin Laden.

There's some lack of agreement over exactly what the military leaders said in the moments before the 2011 operation. In his *Esquire* profile of the Navy SEAL who shot bin Laden, journalist Phil Bronstein reported that just prior to the mission, Admiral William McRaven, who succeeded McChrystal as head of the Joint Special Operations Command, gave "an awesome speech" in which he referenced *Hoosiers*. But other accounts dispute this. In *No Easy Day*, a former SEAL writing under the pseudonym Mark Owen reported that McRaven's final talk was entirely strategic and unmemorable. "Nothing he said stuck with me, as my mind focused on what was about to happen," Owen writes.

To sort this out, I requested interviews with McRaven, Bronstein, and Owen; each declined or didn't respond. However, an officer present at the final mission briefing in Afghanistan offered clarification: It turns out both stories are true. Most of the pre-mission briefing was focused on the strategic game plan, but McRaven did refer to *Hoosiers* during the talk.

"He referenced the scene in which Gene Hackman brings the players into the large arena [for the state championship game]," the officer said. According to this account, McRaven recalled how Coach Dale had one of the players measure the distance from the foul line to the basket ("fifteen feet"), and the height of the rim from the floor ("ten feet"), demonstrating that the arena's court is the same as their home gym's. "He went on to tell the team this mission was no different than any other mission they had done before, and that we would treat it just like another game," this source said. It wasn't a particularly emotional speech, and if anything, it urged the SEAL operators to tamp down their emotions and maintain their usual businesslike demeanor.

That approach seemed to work. During the ninety-minute helicopter flight to bin Laden's compound, most of the SEAL operators were so relaxed that they fell asleep.

5.

The SEALs aren't the only ones who tend to avoid the classic emotional pep talk. Many of the most celebrated modern sports coaches believe locker-room speeches are a cinematic contrivance, not a real-world tool.

Here's how writer David Halberstam describes New England Patriots' coach Bill Belichick, who rarely gives fiery locker-room speeches: "He was driven by his brain power and by his fascination with the challenge that professional football represented to the mind of the coach . . . He was much less skilled than [his mentor, Bill] Parcells at reaching his players emotionally and thereby challenging them to do more. This never came naturally to him; it was not who he was. In addition, he thought it was the wrong way to go, that it was too short-range, and that in the end you could only go to that emotional well so often, and then it went dry."

Here's how eleven-time NBA champion Phil Jackson describes what he learned while playing with the New York Knicks in the 1970s: "At that time most coaches subscribed to the Knute Rockne theory of mental training. They tried to get their players revved up for the game with win-one-for-the-Gipper-style pep talks. That approach may work if you're a linebacker. But what I discovered playing for the Knicks is that when I got too excited mentally, it had a negative effect on my ability to stay focused under pressure. So [as a coach] I did the opposite. Instead of charging players up, I've developed a number of strategies to help them quiet their minds and go into battle poised and in control."

There's not much academic research that tries to determine whether an emotional or information-rich, strategic pep talk is more effective. But much of what we do know about the power of pregame rhetoric comes from a former soccer player turned academic named Tiffanye Vargas.

Vargas grew up in El Paso, Texas, and played on a competitive soccer team. During the regular season, her team often cruised to easy victories, but they'd encounter tougher competition in the playoffs. So before important games, her coach would try to fire them up by talking about how good the other team was.

The coach meant well. Perhaps she thought emphasizing the

other team's prowess would make her players rise to the occasion. Whatever the intentions, this strategy backfired. "All we heard was 'The other team is awesome,'" Vargas recalls. "More often than not, it left us afraid. We lost games when we shouldn't have."

Looking back, Vargas sums up her old coach's pregame speeches simply: "I don't believe she had a clue."

When Vargas began studying psychology at the University of Texas, she started looking for academic research on what kinds of pep talks really work. She found very little. So over the next decade, while earning a PhD in sports psychology at Michigan State, she set out to do the research herself.

In all, she's published a half dozen studies. Some of the results are inconsistent and seemingly contradictory, partly because the methodologies differ. In a lab experiment, for instance, she played one of three different versions of a taped pregame speech to ninety soccer players, to try to determine whether a strategy-focused, information-rich pep talk or an emotionally persuasive approach would leave the team with higher levels of team efficacy. (In this case, the emotional approach left the players feeling more confident and optimistic.) In a field experiment, she surveyed 151 soccer players on ten teams immediately after the teams heard their coaches' real-life pregame speeches. In contrast to the first paper, this time the players who heard speeches that contained more informational content reported feeling higher self-efficacy.

Despite the inconsistencies, some of the findings in Vargas's research are useful. For instance, in one study she found that 90 percent of players enjoy listening to coaches' pregame speeches, 65 percent said it impacted the way they performed in a game, and when players were dissatisfied or asked to critique a coach's pregame speech, the most consistent request was for the coach to be more emotional. (Female athletes, however, show a general preference for more informational speeches.) Across different sports, athletes prefer a pep talk that's information rich if they're playing an unknown opponent or a team to whom they've narrowly lost in the past, and a more emotional pep talk if they're an underdog or playing in a championship game.

Vargas, now at the University of California, Long Beach, would like to find a way to quantify the duration of the effect a good pregame speech can have: Does it help players perform better only during the opening minutes of a game, or is it longer lasting? She'd also like to study how coaches' pregame speeches evolve over the course of a season.

In fact, Barry Staw, a psychology professor at the University of California, Berkeley, has tracked coaches' speeches across a season. Staw is a basketball nut: at age sixty-nine, he still plays full-court pickup games. In the mid-1990s, Staw and a graduate student decided to study the halftime speeches of high school basketball coaches. In all, they corralled twenty-three coaches who taped their talks at 321 games. "There's a huge range of behavior, a lot of very heated rhetoric," Staw says, describing how he used to listen to the talks at home while cooking dinner until his wife outlawed the practice due to all the profanity.

Staw's had coders rate each speech on how strongly it contained nineteen different emotions. The researchers combined these numbers to come up with a single score that captured how "unpleasant" the coach had been in his halftime speech. Then they looked at each team's won-loss record, the record of their opponent in each game, the score at halftime, and the final score.

The primary finding: Teams whose coaches give a really unpleasant, angry halftime speech perform better in the second half.

There are a couple of qualifiers. First, an angry halftime speech has more effect if the coach isn't normally very angry. Second, the effect is curvilinear, meaning the upward slope of the results eventually turns down. More anger doesn't directly equal more performance. "When the coaches start screaming and swearing and breaking trophies and throwing chairs, that does have a negative effect," says Katy DeCelles, a University of Toronto professor who's collaborated with Staw.

Even twenty years after making the recordings, Staw recalls some of the speeches. "One was particularly inspirational. It was better than *Hoosiers*," he says. "It turns out it was given by a coach who went on to run a major college program, and I also learned he had a history in the clergy." Others weren't so uplifting. They were nasty, even frightening. "There were a number that were bone chilling," Staw says, recalling one female coach's talk that left him shaken.

Staw sees anecdotal support for his angry-pep-talks-work-better theory in the world of business. "It probably applies to Steve Jobs," he says, recalling reports of the Apple founder's notorious temper tantrums. "You could argue that a product development team is kind of like a basketball team, and [Jobs's outbursts] did have a particular kind of performance aspect." Still, he believes if a coach's speeches are always angry, they lose their impact. "There is a role for arousal in getting some sort of peak performance, but you only have a certain number of bullets, and you have to allocate them appropriately," he says.

Both Staw's and Vargas's findings suggest that leaders who show emotion during pep talks, and who appeal to their audience's emotions, can be effective and lift the group's performance. But Vargas's results suggest that many audiences want something more than emotion. In many circumstances, an information-rich pep talk may be more effective.

Trying to combine the two approaches could result in a long, cumbersome pep talk. Vargas suggests that's a bad idea: In her view, the best pep talks are short and simple. "Remind your athletes of their strengths," she says. "Don't overload them with new content. This is the time to remind them of whatever key concepts you've been working on during the week in practice. Give them a boost. Tell them something that shows you believe in them. Make them know that they're capable."

6.

When Erica Galos Alioto managed smaller sales teams at Yelp, she didn't rely on formal pep talks. Instead, she led team-building exercises to get everyone energized to sell. They'd sit at tables and pound them like drums. In a favorite drill, she'd ask her reps to stand in a circle and take turns performing a self-designed, silly kung fu move—a trick she learned from an improv class.

"In improv, you warm up so that when you get up there on stage, you're not nervous or anxious," she says. "A lot of reps get really anxious about getting on the phones, and the more we can do to warm them up, the better they're going to be."

Once her teams reached a certain size, she couldn't be so interactive. At first, she tried talking from bullet points, but the results were inconsistent. So she took a full day of training on public speaking. Now she writes a script and practices until she knows the gist of it, then delivers it from memory.

For her August LDOM pep talk to the New York office, she began preparing three weeks in advance, writing a draft and rehearsing on her own. Then, the day before the talk, she asked two senior colleagues to critique her presentation. "I told them very specifically: 'I don't want to just hear that it was great—I want very specific feedback about what could be improved," she says. They told her she was cramming in too many points, so she cut back two sections and streamlined. And she practiced some more.

Although Alioto appears naturally gifted at speaking in front of a large crowd, she's not. She gets nervous. Before a big presentation, she uses a technique she learned in her training. She goes alone into a room. She jumps around energetically. She yells out loud: "You're going to be so excited about what I'm about to tell you! It's going to be amazing! I'm going to blow your mind." She describes this sheepishly. "It's very embarrassing. . . . But I've learned tricks to get past the anxiety."

Most of her sales talks use a simple format, one that's a variation of the formula Stanley McChrystal used with his soldiers. She starts by thanking the team for their hard work, and singling out people who are crushing it. She emphasizes that if one Yelp salesperson can put up spectacular numbers, all the reps are capable of it, since they have similar skills and training. Then she offers up insight on a basic informational concept—often dealing with having the right mentality, or goal setting, or having a commitment to act. "I try to get some response from the audience, and then recap." Her recap isn't just a summary. It's a rallying cry aimed at leaving the group energized.

She's tried angry pep talks, but they don't work for her. (She cites research suggesting women have a hard time using anger as a motivational device.) She abandoned the angry tone not only because it was ineffective, but because of her evolving views on why salespeople aren't successful. She used to blame lack of success on laziness or low engagement, things that naturally made her angry. Instead, she came to see poor results as resulting more from anxiety, lack of confidence or energy, or self-doubt. Instead of reacting critically, she began expressing empathy—"We've all been there"—and offering informational tools to help.

There is surprisingly little academic research into managerial pep talks, but what does exist fits in nicely Alioto's approach. This research describes a concept called Motivating Language Theory, which suggests that leaders giving a pep talk use three kinds of rhetoric.

First is direction-giving or "uncertainty-reducing language"—useful information about *how* to do the task at hand. When Erica Alioto describes how sales reps can reduce negative self-talk, she's reducing the uncertainty people may feel about how to do their job. This mode of communication focuses on the *what* or *how* of the task at hand.

The second type of communication is "meaning-making language"—which explains why this task is important. When coaches or managers emphasize the importance of team or family or the legacy of the institution, they're engaged in meaning making.

Third is "empathetic language," which shows concern for the

performer as an individual and a human. Praise, encouragement, and thanks fall under this heading.

Much of the research into Motivating Language Theory has been done by Jacqueline and Milton Mayfield at Texas A&M. "MLT provides a framework for understanding how leader communication can invigorate and activate people toward achieving desired organizational goals, as well as their own," Jacqueline said by e-mail.

It's a conceptual theory, and there's not an easy or obvious way to prove or test it scientifically. But in a 1998 study of salespeople tasked with selling ads for university telephone directories, researchers Theodore Zorn and Sarah Ruccio found real-world results that more or less jive with the theoretical model. Based on interviews with reps and managers, they found that communication in three areas were most valued by reps: modeling success (which sounds a lot like direction giving), individualized attention (which is empathetic communication), and exuding energy.

At Yelp's New York office, Alioto's pep talk doesn't really end when the salespeople file back to their desks. During her formal remarks, she'd asked every salesperson to write a goal for the day on a Post-it note, and she'd set her own Post-it goal: to talk individually with at least one hundred Yelp salespeople. After her speech, Alioto grabbed a soy latte and began walking the floor to talk one-on-one with her team.

Observing a dozen or so of these conversations, what's striking is to me is how much they focus on information and strategy. She talks to one rep about how to more forcefully move an ambivalent prospect into completing the order. For a salesperson who's about to call an automobile mechanic, she talks about the specifics of that category: Since mechanics rely so heavily on referrals, Yelp drives more business to them than to, say, restaurants. "I love mechanics. The ROI [return on investment] is so easy to explain," she says.

As Alioto wanders the sales floor, music plays overhead, and the noise level periodically cranks up as a salesperson bangs the bong. At 2 P.M., aka Power Hour, Yelpers rush the kitchen to grab from the free supply of Red Bull to prevent the postlunch lull.

By day's end, Alioto has talked with at least a hundred reps. The team has a good day: They sell $1.45 million in new ads, meeting their quota but falling $50,000 short of that month's stretch target. Many reps achieve BME, Yelpspeak for "best month ever."

It's impossible to say how much of those results have been influenced by Alioto's morning remarks, or the one-on-one pep talks that followed. Nonetheless, the sales leader felt the day was successful. "[My speech] wasn't anything groundbreaking, but it helped them think about where they are and what they are capable of in a different way," she says. "We all can get into our own heads sometimes and set limitations for ourselves. I try to make everyone understand that they have the power to control their day."

It may lack the poetry or cinematic appeal of "Let's win one for the Gipper." But by calibrating the right mix of information and emotion, the Yelp sales team was energized for LDOM. (All that Red Bull probably helped, too.) And amid the polished concrete floors and exposed ceiling beams of a high-tech workplace, this counts as a win.

Chapter Four

CREATING A PERFORMANCE PLAYLIST

*WHAT'S THE PERFECT SONG TO HELP
YOU ENERGIZE AND FOCUS?*

TJ Connelly was not an athletic child. Growing up south of Boston, he participated in school theatrical productions. He tried to play the drums, the clarinet, and the bass guitar, with limited success. By the time TJ was in high school in the early 1990s, he'd become a serious music fan, favoring bands like Ministry. While some classmates impressed girls with athletic prowess, Connelly had a different go-to move: If he liked a girl, he'd make her a mixtape.

Connelly also liked computers. After graduating from high school in 1995, the Internet was just beginning to boom, so Connelly skipped college and became a programmer. For a few years, money fell from the sky. But then the bubble burst. To make ends meet, he took a job as a bouncer at a college bar. There he spent long hours watching over the dance floor, and he found himself paying close attention to the DJ. "He's drinking for free, all the girls are talking to him, and he's playing superloud music," Connelly says. "I was like, well, that's better than my gig." So he decided to become a DJ.

He worked some weddings, but his primary job was at a 200-seat improv theater in the North End. Unlike playing music in a dance club or at a wedding, where DJs have plenty of time to plan the right song-by-song sequences, playing songs for improv helped Connelly develop quick reflexes and encyclopedic musical knowledge. "It's really about being able to connect a spontaneous live event with a random musical connection," he says. For instance, if the actors on stage improvise their way into a scene that involves driving a car, Connelly might quickly queue up a snippet from the Beatles' "Drive My Car" or the Cars' "Drive." To prepare, he'd spend long hours "making bumps"—that is, capturing the perfect few seconds of a song (often the chorus), so that when he hits PLAY, the audience hears just the right lyrics. Over the next few years, Connelly spun songs at hundreds of nights of improv.

Around this time, in the early 2000s, Connelly attended a Red Sox game at Fenway Park. He noticed music playing over the loudspeakers. He asked around, and found out that Fenway Park had its own DJ. "What a cool job," he thought. So he sent a letter to the Red Sox detailing his experience as a DJ. He received no reply, but the following spring, he sent another letter. Sending the letter became an annual ritual. Then, in 2005, before he had a chance to mail it, the Red Sox called. They wanted him to audition to become the backup DJ. He went to a game, sat in the booth, and in the fourth inning, the current DJ asked him to take over. Connelly felt comfortable: It wasn't much different than playing music for a 200-seat theater, except that Fenway seated 33,000. A month later, Connelly heard he'd become the Sox backup DJ, remaining on call in case the regular DJ called in sick. In 2008, he became the first-string DJ. By 2015, he'd worked more than five hundred games as Fenway Park's musical director.

The job involves playing music in four different scenarios. Several hours before the game, he chooses the music the Red Sox players hear during batting practice, tailoring his song choices to each player's musical preferences. During the game, he spins each player's "walk-up" music, a few seconds of a song as the player approaches home plate to bat. (Most players choose their own walk-up songs, but sometimes Connelly makes recommendations or uses his discretion to choose the right section of a song.) Between innings, when Fenway's organist isn't playing, Connelly plays songs to try to keep the crowd energized. And after key plays, he'll quickly play "situationals," snippets of music to celebrate a home run or a big defensive play. If the Sox turn a double play, for instance, he might quickly punch up Rob Base and DJ E-Z Rock's "It Takes Two." If an opposing pitcher throws a wild pitch, Connelly may mock him with a few bars from "Wild Thing."

Connelly, who is 37, describes his role in a game this way:

"There's energy that comes from the players on the field and back to the crowd, and my job is to be the amplifier in between them. . . . If something good happens in the game, you build on that. If something bad happens, you try to move back away from it. It's basically like making a mixtape. You take the high songs and the low songs, and you try to create this feeling so that nothing is jarring. It's all about the tone."

By all accounts, Connelly is very good at what he does—so much so that in 2013, an executive from the New England Patriots football team asked, "Why can't our music be more like the music at Fenway?" So the Patriots hired Connelly as a special consultant. He attended a few games and wrote a memo. (His key message: Play a wider variety of songs.) Then the Patriots asked Connelly to DJ a single game on November 24, 2013.

The opponent was the Denver Broncos, and the game was being televised on *Sunday Night Football*. The Patriots fumbled on their first three possessions. With two minutes left in the first half, the Pats were down 24-0. The crowd was dead silent.

Looking out from the DJ booth, Connelly said to the production staff, "We need to get these people dancing." The producers mocked him: In miserable weather and with the fans booing the hometown team, that's simply not possible. Connelly smiled, queued up Daft Punk's "Get Lucky," and turned up the volume. Connelly could see the wave of recognition—"Oh, it's *that* song"—ripple through the stands. People stood up. Many began singing along. Some danced. "It was perfect," Connelly says, smiling the way he often does when recalling a moment when he played the perfect song. After halftime, with Connelly spinning songs to keep the crowd on its feet, the Patriots began an epic comeback, ultimately winning on an overtime field goal. A few days after the game, a Patriots' executive approached Connelly: "Maybe you'd like to come back?"

In 2014, Connelly became the Patriots' permanent DJ, while keeping the Fenway Park gig, too. A few months later, the Patriots won their fourth Super Bowl of the Tom Brady-Bill Belichick era. There is no proof that Connelly's choice of music had anything to do with the team's success that season. But the music is a key element in creating crowd noise and supporting the environment that gives the team its home-field advantage. As anyone who's experienced that mysterious alchemy when just the right song comes on at just the right time can attest, it surely doesn't hurt.

2.

Getting psyched up is a process of calibrating emotions and adrenaline. There are tools to help. Rituals and superstition, discussed in Chapter Two, are one example. So are pep talks, as described in Chapter Three.

Music is probably the most ubiquitous tool that performers—especially athletes—use to get ready to compete. Watch a football team (whether NFL or high school) get off the bus, and most players will be wearing headphones. At NBA games, players wear wireless headphones during pregame shootarounds. Many athletes listen to carefully curated playlists of songs designed to motivate, inspire, and energize.

They are hardly the first people to realize that music can have a beneficial impact on performance. Music has been a part of warfare since the days of the Etruscans, Teutons, and Celts, with drums providing a cadence to march to and a signal to attack. During the Civil War, the Northern and Southern armies employed tens of thousands of musicians. In 2014, the U.S. Department of Defense remained the single largest employer of musicians in America, with more than six thousand musicians on its payroll.

But in the last fifteen years, the scientific study of exactly how and why music can help people perform better has become far more extensive and robust. That's largely due to technology—iPods, smartphones, iTunes, and streaming music services—but that isn't the only factor. Much of the scientific outpouring has been driven by the energetic work of a single researcher named Costas Karageorghis.

Karageorghis grew up in South London, in a flat above a used-record store. Each morning he'd wake to the thumping bass resonating up from the store below. As a child, he played a variety of musical instruments and he ran track. At college, he decided to combine his two passions. Now a researcher at Brunel University in London, Karageorghis is the world's foremost expert on the interplay between music and physical performance. He's published more than a hundred scientific papers, written three books (including *Applying Music in Exercise and Sport*), and consulted for companies including Nike and the global sports agency IMG.

He wasn't the first to study how music affects athletic performance. He describes a study from 1911 that examined how music from a brass band affected competitors in a New York City bicycle race. But until Karageorghis began his work in the mid-1990s, the field was characterized by researchers who'd do just a study or two and then move to a new topic, and it was plagued by poor methodology. Karageorghis moved the field forward by creating a conceptual framework for how motivational music helps people perform, and then constructing a survey instrument that allowed people to quantify what types of songs they found motivational. He and a colleague also published a two-part "synthesis and review" in which they examined every piece of published research on music and exercise.

Anyone who's tried to build his own playlist can benefit from understanding how scientists determine what kind of music is motivational, and exactly how it drives performance. For instance, the papers distinguish between music that's listened to "pretask" (say, in the locker room before a game), "during task" (during a spinning session or on headphones during a marathon), and "posttask" (while recuperating after an event). The research also distinguishes between the effects of music during "exercise" (a physical activity aimed at improving health) and "sport" (an activity featuring rules and a competitive outcome, that may or may not involve a large amount of physical exertion). Different kinds of songs may work better or worse in these different contexts.

The research tries to tease out exactly what it is about a piece of music that makes it motivational. It focuses on four components: its rhythm and tempo (measured by, among other things, beats per minute), its musicality (the melody and harmony), its cultural impact (its pervasiveness or general perception in society), and its association (that is, how an individual links a song to a certain life experience, memory, or media representation). The first two qualities, rhythm and musicality, are "intrinsic" qualities that stem directly from the music itself; the latter two are functions of how a piece of music exists within culture, and will differ from person to person. In Karageorghis's model, rhythm and musicality are the most important drivers of a song's motivational quality; cultural impact and association are less important. Although academics use a tool to create a numeric score of how motivational a song is, it's not an objective measurement; different people will find different songs more or less motivational.

"The key to a motivational track is that it physically energizes, stimulates, and activates," Karageorghis says. "A piece of music can do this on many different levels. It has to do with tempo or speed. It might have to do with rhythm or accentuation, or melody and lyrical content. . . . Music may also be motivational through a process of classical conditioning, so that a piece of music is associated with motivational imagery." One of the best examples of that, Karageorghis says, is the music from the *Rocky* movies; when people hear the songs, they recollect the motivational training montages, and this memory arouses and energize them.

So if someone is working out and a highly motivating song comes on, what happens? One effect is synchronization, particularly if she's engaged in a rhythmic activity such as running, rowing, or cycling: a song with the right beats per minute can help pace her movements (steps, strokes) through a workout. (Research by Heather Hoffmann of Knox College has shown this is also true for people who listen to music during sex: The beats per minute of a song affect thrusts per minute during intercourse.) The right music can also improve an exerciser's mood. It can assist with arousal control, keeping the athlete "up" and energized, or calm and collected. It can create a sense of dissociation or distraction, in which the athlete's mind drifts away from the unpleasant sensations of exercise. (This only works up to moderate intensity; nothing can distract someone from a *really* hard workout.) It can reduce a person's sense of "perceived exertion"—meaning she will feel like she's working less hard than she really is. And beyond perceptions, study after study has shown that motivational music can lead to measurably better output and better performance in a variety of exercise settings.

"In a sense, music can be thought of as a type of legal performance-enhancing drug," Karaeorghis and his coauthor, David-Lee Priest, write in one study.

To make use of this drug, Karageorghis suggests that athletes break a workout into different components, such as a stretching, warm-up, mental preparation components, and strength, endurance, and cooldown components, and create special playlists for each one, recognizing how different motivational songs will work better in different places. For rhythmic exercises like running, beats per minute are important, and there are Web sites to help people choose music whose tempo matches the pace they hope to set. Distraction and disassociation may be more important during a grueling endurance or interval training workout; slower, more sedate music can assist with cooldown.

Karageorghis, who continues to run, does this himself. During stretching and warm-ups, he listens to up-tempo tracks from artists like Pharrell Williams and Justin Timberlake, and he often circles back to music that was popular when he was a teenager, such as Michael Jackson, because it reminds him of his formative years as an athlete. He doesn't listen to music while he runs, but during cooldown, he'll switch to jazz pianist Oscar Peterson or some Miles Davis.

Like any tool, music can be misused and actually hinder performance. For instance, many athletes listen to music while training even though the sports in which they participate don't allow music during competition. Running is an example: Serious competitions forbid competitors from wearing headphones. This breaks the cardinal rule of "practice like you'll play." Karageorghis also sees too many athletes listening to suboptimal playlists; for instance, many people listen to entire albums by the same artist while exercising, even though the tempo and emotional association differ dramatically from one song to the next. Or he'll see an athlete who's prone to nervousness or anxiety listening to highly arousing, stimulating music (for example, the Black Eyed Peas) before a competition, when something that's likely to be energizing but a bit less agitating (such as Enigma, or even a classical piece) might be better.

In a few years, Karageorghis hopes to understand even more about how music can help drive performance. Most of what we know to date is based on behavioral experiments, in which people listen to different types of music (and a control group listens to no music at all), perform different activities, and are closely measured, monitored, and compared. That doesn't give researchers a window into what's happening in their brains at a neural level, and that's what Karageorghis hopes to someday discover. "Ultimately what I need is a functional MRI machine that can be used in an exercise environment," he says. "That would really open up this field and allow me to answer the burning questions." He hopes that technology may be available in the 2020s.

3.

Karageorghis's reference to the music from *Rocky* as a motivational masterpiece isn't a random example. The *Rocky* theme songs are referenced repeatedly in research on motivational music. For instance, in one 1995 study, two researchers asked pairs of runners who'd posted equal speeds in the past to compete against each other in the 60-meter dash. Before the athletes ran, however, one group stood in silence. The other group listened to the theme from *Rocky* on headphones. Afterward, the *Rocky* listeners ran faster. Their heartbeats were quicker, their muscles were tenser, and their anxiety was lower. Listening to just one minute of the *Rocky* theme song gave them a significant and systematic physiological advantage.

That phenomenon brought me to a large home in suburban Chicago, where I'm welcomed inside by a sixty-four-year-old man. The front of his black hair is dyed bright purple. He's wearing a tight leather jacket over a tight chartreuse T-shirt, black acid-washed jeans, and custom-made purple ostrich boots. Around his neck is a gigantic silver pendant of an electric guitar. It looks like he's dressed to perform at a rock concert, but in fact he has nothing special going on. He dresses like a rock star every day. "I like to stand out," he says, describing how he employs a tailor who custom-makes his leather clothing.

Jim Peterik can afford his own leatherworker—as well as the 182 guitars he keeps at home— for a simple reason, one he demonstrates on a white grand piano just off the dining room. He begins playing a familiar series of pounding chords. The song is called "Eye of the Tiger," and Peterik, who played guitar and keyboards for the band Survivor in the 1980s, cowrote the tune in 1981.

At the time, Survivor had made a couple of albums and was touring clubs, but it was a struggle. Then Peterik received a message on his answering machine from Sylvester Stallone, who was looking for a theme song for *Rocky III*. The first two Rocky movies featured orchestral scores by Bill Conti, who won an Oscar for this work. By the early 1980s, Stallone wanted a rock sound track to better appeal to young moviegoers. A music producer friend had played Stallone one of Survivor's early albums, and he loved the crashing power chords and the strong backbeat.

Stallone sent Peterik and his writing partner, Survivor guitarist Frankie Sullivan, the first three minutes of *Rocky III*. It contained an opening montage that introduces the character Clubber Lang (played by the unknown actor Mr. T) and shows how Rocky has gotten soft and rich, filming TV commercials instead of training. The scenes were set to the Queen song "Another One Bites the Dust," but Stallone couldn't convince Queen to license the rights. The songwriters looked at each other. "How are we going to top that?"

On his guitar, Peterik began playing the same note in metronomic sixteenths, a sound he calls "digga-digga-digga-digga," which is meant to simulate the jittery heartbeat of someone who's excited. Stopping and starting the film, they worked out a series of abrupt chord changes timed precisely to the punches in the opening boxing scene. Then they stalled out. Since they'd viewed only three minutes of film, they didn't know enough about the story to write lyrics, so they begged Stallone to send the entire movie. Grudgingly, he did.

As Peterik and Sullivan watched the complete film, the pivotal moment came in a scene after Rocky has lost a fight to Clubber Lang, and his longtime manager, Mickey, has died. While Rocky reflects in a darkened gym where he once trained, Apollo Creed, his opponent in the first two *Rocky* movies, enters and offers his analysis of why Rocky lost. "When we fought, you had the eye of the tiger, man, the edge. Now you gotta get it back, and the way to get it back is to go back to the beginning," Apollo says. "Maybe we could win it back together. Eye of the tiger, man."

Peterik and Sullivan started writing lyrics around the phrase. As an opening line, Sullivan suggested: "Back on the street, doing time, taking chances." Peterik explained to me how he rewrote and expanded that snippet to become: "Rising up, back on the street, did my time, took my chances. Went the distance, now

I'm back on the street, just a man, and his will to survive." "That came like one lump, pretty much," he recalls. At the time, Peterik was a jogger, so over the next few days he jogged around his neighborhood in La Grange, Illinois, stopping to write down song lyrics on a notepad he kept in his gym shorts. A few days later, the band convened at a Chicago studio to record a demo. Stallone loved it.

The band rented tuxedos to attend the Hollywood premier in May 1982, but it wasn't until the film opened back home in La Grange that Peterik realized how big the song could be. "It was the second day *Rocky III* was in theaters, and the place was packed. I sat in the back row all alone. When the song hit, the place went up like a rock concert."

It was just the right song, at just the right moment.

"Eye of the Tiger" hit number one and won a Grammy, which sits upstairs in Peterik's home recording studio. It made Survivor famous, and they followed with up with a series of hits: "I Can't Hold Back," "High on You," "Burning Heart," "The Search Is Over."

When I interviewed Peterick, "Eye of the Tiger" was thirty-three years old, and Peterik tries to explain what makes it the most iconic psych-up song of all time. He rejects the notion that it's entirely because of the *Rocky* tie-in: Since iTunes launched in 2001, "Eye of the Tiger" has been downloaded nearly six million times, and Peterik argues that many of the people buying the song today are too young to have watched *Rocky III*. He's arguing, in the language of the academic theorists, that the song's appeal is due to its intrinsic musicality, not just to its emotional association with an uplifting movie.

Peterik believes the unusually long intro is a key. Most rock songs jump to the lyrics quickly, but this intro lasts more than thirty seconds, with the combination of the digga-diggas and the power chords give listeners a period in which they can get excited for the lyrics that follow. The lyrics, which focus on struggle, conflict, and rivalry, could apply to any range of performance pursuits. "They're very anthemic words," he says.

Today rehab hospitals use "Eye of the Tiger" to motivate stroke victims undergoing physical therapy. He's talked with CEOs who listen to it before board meetings. In a *New York* magazine essay about her pregnancy, one woman recalled how she had her doctor play the song at the precise moment she was artificially inseminated, to psych her uterus up to conceive.

The songwriter admits that if he knew exactly what it was about "Eye of the Tiger" that keeps it on so many workout playlists, he'd have had more luck writing another song like it. In fact, Stallone asked him to write the theme for *Rocky IV*, but "Burning Heart" didn't catch on as widely.

"There's something in the DNA of 'Eye of the Tiger' that I wish I could clone," he says. "It's just magic."

4.

Compared with a motivational tool like a pep talk, music has a distinct advantage: Depending on the type of performance you're doing, you may be able to continue listening to it *while* you perform, not just beforehand. That's particularly true if you're engaged in office work, where the right kind of music can help you remain focused and energized.

This isn't a new idea. Factory managers first began trying to use music to enhance the productivity of workers nearly a century ago, their interest sparked by the scientific management movement known as Taylorism and the development of electronic public address systems that allowed people to broadcast music in a large facility. In those early days, companies tended to play upbeat music to keep workers working briskly. In fact, long before it became synonymous with elevator music, Muzak built a large and successful business creating productivity music that it delivered on records to factories.

In the twenty-first century, people listen to music at work differently. Instead of managers selecting the songs, workers choose the music themselves, and generally play it on headphones. But does this really make people work harder, better, or smarter?

The answer is: It depends.

Anneli Haake earned a doctorate in music psychology at the

University of Sheffield, and her dissertation focused on the use of music in office settings. Based on her own research and the research of others, she created a flowchart that suggests whether music is going to help a person perform better at work. She starts with a person's personality and preferences: Is the person an introvert or extrovert? (Extroverts are better at working while listening to music; introverts are more likely to find it distracting.) Did the person grow up in a home where music was often on in the background? What is the person's attitude toward silence? Does she find it peaceful, or does she complain about an environment being "too quiet"?

Next she looks at situational factors. Even the least distracting music—say, a lyricless classical composition a person has never heard before—consumes some amount of a listener's "attention capacity," even if he's not trying to listen to it. So Haake looks at how much attention capacity the person has, the complexity of the task he's doing, and his familiarity and confidence at performing the task, among other factors. All else equal, if you're an extrovert, you don't like silence, and if the work you're doing is very familiar and you're good at it, music is more likely to be beneficial. If you're an introvert who favors the Amtrak Quiet Car and you're studying for a physics class in which you currently have a C-minus, it's probably best to put away the iPod.

But that analysis ignores one huge factor: the acoustic environment in which you're working. If everyone worked in an office as quiet as a library, music might be less essential. In our cubicle-ized world, wearing headphones is largely about blocking out other kinds of distracting noise, as well as signaling "Do not disturb" to colleagues. Haake's research suggests that a lot of the people who work with headphones on are probably having their concentration interrupted, at least slightly, by the music, but they're *less* distracted by music than by the environmental noise. (In other words, the music is the lesser of two evils.) This scenario is, in fact, the way Haake works herself: Since she's somewhat introverted and much of her work involves writing (a complex task), she prefers to work in silence. But if she's working someplace noisy, she'll wear head-phones and play music.

There's little research on what kinds of music work best to put workers into a flow state, but there are anecdotal rules of thumb. Lyrics sap attention, so lyricless music is better. Familiar tunes are likely to make your mind wander, so vaguely unrecognizable music is a superior choice. And headphones are a must: A man-ager who thinks he can make workers more productive by choos-ing and broadcasting music to the entire office is almost certainly fooling himself. "The main thing that came out for me in my study was that it has to be a personal choice. If the music is not a personal choice, it can actually have a negative impact," Haake says.

To find out what songs large numbers of people use to get psyched or to focus, the best place to turn is Spotify, the streaming music service that currently has more than 1.5 billion user-created

playlists on its site. Most of the lists are geared to particular contexts. People create playlists for commuting. Or for dinner parties. Or for "sexy time." Within a general category, there are often
multiple subcategories: Among workout playlists, for instance,
there are some for walking, spinning, jogging, CrossFit, strength
training, or yoga.

Paul Lamere is director of platform development at the Echo
Nest, a Spotify subsidiary that analyzes how users choose music.
Sitting in his office one day, I ask Lamere to find playlists for psyching up. It's a use case he hasn't considered before, so he plays with
his computer. "We have golf prep, football prep, so yes, people are
definitely creating playlists for this." I suggest he search for playlists using the word "psych or "psyched." There's a long pause. "Oh,
yeah," he says. "There's 'Locker-room psych.' There's 'Get psyched.'
There's a lot of them, in fact." He quickly aggregates the data, finding the songs most likely to be in a psych-up playlist. The list is
dominated by 1980s rock: Bon Jovi, Van Halen, Kiss, Poison, Journey, Mötley Crüe, and Guns N' Roses all have songs in the top
twenty.

He ponders the list. To his mind, they suggest forty-year-old
guys choosing songs for workouts, songs that, in most cases, were
popular when they were teenagers. It's not so much the lyrics that
make these good songs for getting psyched up, he says, as the heavy
guitar riffs and the high energy.

Personally, I can't imagine Poison's "Talk Dirty to Me" helping

me mentally prepare for *anything,* but it's apparent from both research and anecdote that the right music for mental preparation
is a very personal choice.

Consider a story told by a high-level administrator at a pres-
tigious East Coast college. In 2005, he was interviewing for a chief
marketing officer job at a large company, and he was invited to
give a presentation on the company's marketing strategy to the
CEO and ten other top executives. Earlier in the hiring process,
he'd learned the search had narrowed to him and one other final-
ist, and that the other guy had been offered the job but turned it
down. Now the company had come back to my acquaintance as
the second choice. "It was clear there were some people in the
group who really wanted to hire me, and some people who really
didn't want to hire me, so they were going to grill me," he recalls.

Sitting in the parking lot before the meeting, he put on a song
he'd specially chosen for this moment: "Boogie Shoes," by KC and
the Sunshine Band. "It's this preening 1970s disco tune," he says,
one he recalled from high school dances. "It sort of gave me a
little strut that I took into the room." He nailed the presentation.
After he was hired, a colleague told him he'd never seen someone
command a boardroom the way he had. The college administrator declined to let me use his name because he finds the story
embarrassing, but no matter how silly he looked rocking out to
KC and the Sunshine Band in the parking lot, he attributes his
stellar performance, in part, to the unusual psych-up song.

In the early 2000s, Amy Perlmutter was working at a state agency that politicians wanted to eliminate, but they lacked the votes to do so. Every few months, she'd be called into tense meetings where the department's haters would criticize her. "It was a ridiculous, no-win situation," she recalls. "I had to really psych myself up to go see them, and the way I did it was I'd put on the sound track from *Annie*. I'd sing along in my office, then I'd try to get my staff to sing along, too." At first Perlmutter recalls choosing songs like "Tomorrow" and "You're Never Fully Dressed Without a Smile" simply because they're upbeat and cheery, but as we talked, she recalled something more specific. She'd seen *Annie* on Broadway with a close friend in high school—a warm and rich visual memory, which may have helped her mood improve before the meetings. "Afterward, I'd walk into the meeting with a big smile and a lot of energy, and I think things ended up being friendlier and more positive because of that."

5.

On a Monday in late April, TJ Connelly enters Fenway Park's production booth at 2:30 P.M., to get ready for batting practice an hour later.

Connelly has flowing dark hair and a long beard. He's dressed in a ratty black golf shirt and gray checked pants. He stands before a Yamaha soundboard, black headphones around his neck, clicking on a laptop that holds more than thirty-five thousand songs. In front of him, a breeze blows in through a large open window, and below, Red Sox players congregate around the batting cage.

A few minutes into batting practice, he's playing rap songs like "Super Disco Breakin'" by the Beastie Boys. Many of these songs contain expletives, so Connelly has painstakingly edited "clean" versions with the profanity excised. He keeps meticulous records of what he plays, to avoid repeating songs too frequently, all the while noting the players' reactions. During today's batting practice they hear nineteen songs by artists including Jay Z, Cypress Hill, and Kendrick Lamar. The visiting team, in contrast, will conduct batting practice to organ music.

Some of the musical cues at Fenway are routinized. Connelly always plays the intro from the TV show Cheers fifty minutes before game time, and "Sweet Caroline" always marks the middle of the eighth inning, with the crowd singing along.

Connelly puts little thought into those preprogrammed choices. Instead, he obsesses over finding songs that fit the tone and moment of game situations. He keeps ready an entire folder of songs for rain delays, including "Here Comes the Rain Again" and "Invisible Sun." He has a song ready in case a fan reaches out from the stands to interfere with a ball in play ("Keep Your Hands to Yourself"), or if a fan jumps onto the field during play ("What Do You Do with a Drunken Sailor?").

Tonight's game quickly gets ugly. Four minutes after the first pitch, the Red Sox are losing by a run; eleven minutes later, they're down by three. There is no music playing, because there's nothing for hometown fans to celebrate.

As each Red Sox player comes to bat, Connelly queues up the batter's walk-up song. The practice of playing specific songs for certain players dates to the 1970s, but according to a history of the practice by Daniel Brown of the *San Jose Mercury News,* it grew rapidly after the 1993 Seattle Mariners began playing a walk-up song for each player. For some stars, the musical introductory number becomes a key part of their identity: A generation of Yankee fans can't hear Metallica's "Enter Sandman" without recalling closer Mariano Rivera's entrance from the bull pen.

Players have different motivations in choosing their walk-up songs. Connelly recalls one player using a Miley Cyrus song, because it made him think of his daughters, and he drew a connection between succeeding at the plate and being able to provide a good life for his family. Some players don't care much about the music and let Connelly play whatever he likes. Connelly recalls relief pitcher Andrew Miller, who didn't express any song preference until Connelly introduced him with a snippet of the Johnny Cash song "God's Gonna Cut You Down." The next day, a call came from the clubhouse: Miller approved of the pick. "That one. Every time. It's perfect."

If Connelly had to choose his own walk-up song, he'd opt for the opening of "I'm on a Boat," by the Lonely Island. Sometimes players ask for suggestions. On the night I visited, David Ortiz had chosen two songs of his own, and directed Connelly to pick a third "dealer's choice"; Connelly chose "The Devil Is a Lie" by Rick Ross and Jay Z. Connelly noticed Ortiz bobbing his head to the song as he approached the plate; apparently, it's a keeper.

As play progresses, Connelly is constantly thinking about songs that might be appropriate for the situation. In the top of the fourth, with the Sox behind, the Blue Jays get two men on, and the atmosphere is tense. The batter tries to bunt. He gets under it, and hits a tiny blooper toward shallow third base. The Sox third base-man lays out to make a spectacular diving, belly-flopping catch. The crowd begins to roar, and less than a second later, the theme song from *Superman* comes over the PA system. The crowd's noise level increases noticeably as they recognize the song and its con-nection to the superhero catch. Along with the higher volume, this cheer takes longer to die down. It's exactly the amplification process Connelly aspires to achieve. Looking down on the crowd, Connelly gives a satisfied smile.

"I sit here waiting for those moments."

In the middle of the eighth inning, the Red Sox are losing to the Blue Jays, 5-4. Connelly plays "Sweet Caroline," turning down the volume during the "so good" chorus so the crowd can take over the vocals. As Connelly turns off the music, the crowd re-mains standing and singing. Even on a chilly night, the right song can bring a crowd to life.

Suddenly, the ballplayers seem to come to life, too. The Red Sox lead off with a single. Connelly cues "Blitzkrieg Bop" by the Ramones. The second batter singles. The runners advance to second and third on a wild pitch. Connelly plays "Wild Thing." The pitcher intentionally walks Ortiz to load the bases, with no outs. The next batter hits a sacrifice fly, knocking in the tying run. Connelly plays "One More Time" by Daft Punk. As the inning ends, he cues up the synth-heavy song "Sandstorm" by the Finnish DJ Darude, the intro song for Red Sox closer Koji Uehara. Earlier in the evening, Connelly had pointed to the volume control on his soundboard, explaining how he's not supposed to push the volume above a certain mark. But with the score tied and the closer walking toward the mound to start the ninth inning, the green lights flicker noticeably above that threshold.

The Blue Jays go down 1-2-3.

In the production booth, there's a quick debate. "I'm Shipping Up to Boston" by the Dropkick Murphys used to be the intro song for Sox closer Jonathan Papelbon. When Papelbon was traded to the Phillies after the 2011 season, the song was retired at Fenway. A year or two later, however, the Red Sox decided to reclaim it: Now Connelly plays the rousing anthem only in the middle of the ninth inning of very close games. With a tie score, Connelly and his boss decide the situation warrants the Dropkick Murphys signature tune. Outside, the crowd of 34,769 is standing and cheering.

In the bottom of the ninth, shortstop Xander Bogaerts hits a one-out single. Then Ryan Hanigan singles. Connelly spins "This Is How We Do It" by Montell Jordan. With runners on first and second, Mookie Betts singles up the middle, scoring the go-ahead run and a walk-off victory. The Red Sox mob Betts as he rounds second base. Connelly hits a button, and the PA system blares "Dirty Water," the song that concludes every Red Sox home win.

Perhaps in a few years, Costas Karageorghis will be able to wheel a functional MRI machine onto this field to do scientific A/B testing to see how well players hit, field, and throw after listening to different kinds of songs, or to no music at all.

Until then, we will draw what lessons we can from both the researchers and the practitioners. We can consider whether rhythm and musicality or emotional associations are more likely to get us excited or keep us calm. We can search out songs that help bring us closer to the magical state of flow.

And if all that fails, we can put on "Eye of the Tiger" and turn up the volume.

Chapter Five

THE KEYS TO CONFIDENCE

*SHOULD YOU RELY ON YOUR CONSCIOUS MIND,
YOUR SUBCONSCIOUS MIND, OR GO ON AUTOPILOT?*

John Quinn, the backup goalie on the West Point lacrosse team, is sitting in an enclosed, egg-shaped chair, listening to an elaborately produced audio track that talks about how great he is.

From inside the chair comes the opening chords of the AC/DC song "Shoot to Thrill." Then a narrator begins to speak: "The time is now and the place is here. . . . This is where I take my game to the next level. . . . I've paid my dues along the way and earned the right to be here. What's important now is to stay charged up and a little bit pissed off."

As Quinn listens to the sound track, Nate Zinsser, the lacrosse team's sports psychologist, watches biofeedback data on a video screen.

During four previous appointments, Zinsser and Quinn had talked about his lacrosse résumé—his career highlights in high school, his strengths and weaknesses, and the skills he needs to improve. Zinsser, who'd been co-captain of his high school lacrosse team and now works at West Point's Center for Enhanced Performance, used those conversations to write the script for this personalized, ten-minute motivational sound track. It's narrated by a voice-over performer kept on retainer by West Point for just this purpose. Today is the first time Quinn is hearing it.

Quinn's imagery sound track continues: "From here on in whenever I think about playing lacrosse, I think about playing great. I accept that the best goalies in the world are going to let in some goals sometimes—but they don't let it bother them. They treat every mistake as temporary, limited and rare. . . . As I look honestly at myself, I think of so many things that I do well, and so many ways I am really good at what I do: The way I had fifteen saves against New York state champions West Islip in my junior year. . . . The way I shut down Smithtown's All-Star attack. . . . Whenever it gets tough, I just remind myself that I am an impact player on a team that's going all the way—it was meant for me, and it was meant for us!"

After a few minutes, Quinn emerges from the egg chair smiling. "I was picturing a lot of the images," he says. "I would see myself throwing the outlet, or watching the shooter come across. When it went into the good memory part of it, I wasn't zoning out. I was locked in, just totally digging it."

Zinsser instructs Quinn to load the track onto his phone and listen to it before every practice and game. Quinn says he's going to play it before going to sleep, as well.

The psychologist, who is sixty-two, with a wiry body and receding gray hair, has appointments like this every hour on the hour, mostly with varsity athletes, but also with army cadets who want to learn techniques to perform better in academics, military duties, or in the rest of their lives. The amount of one-on-one attention he provides is extraordinary. For example, Zinsser estimates he's spent more than fifty hours working individually with the lacrosse team's starting goalie. In offices down the hall, two other PhDs are doing similar work with members of other army teams.

A photo on his office wall recalls the moment when Zinsser became interested in sports psychology. The photo shows him as a 123-pound high school wrestler standing next to an opponent he's just defeated. In that pivotal match, Zinsser was losing with just sixteen seconds left, when he entered what he recalls as an "altered state, out-of-body, in-the-zone moment." Time slowed down, and he suddenly felt all powerful. He was able to execute a takedown of his opponent to win the match. (He eventually won the state championship.) After migrating through a series of coaching jobs in his twenties, Zinsser figured out his goal in life: to help other people learn to enter the high-performance zone that he'd discovered while wrestling.

He earned a PhD in sports psychology from the University of Virginia, where he studied under Bob Rotella, whose psychological techniques are well known in golf. Zinsser was working at a state university in Pennsylvania in 1992 when West Point recruited him away. When he's not working with cadets, who call him "Doc Z," he works with professional athletes (his office wall contains a collection of autographed "Thank you" photos) and practices martial arts.

West Point began its foray into sports psychology in the late 1980s, when one of its football coaches thought better mental preparation might help Army's placekickers better handle the pressure of making last-second, game-winning kicks. Under Zinsser's guidance, the program expanded. Today the Center for Enhanced Performance offers tutoring and classes on study skills and performance psychology, but much of its work resembles what Zinsser has spent the last hour doing with the backup goalie: teaching cadets to use visualization, relaxation techniques, affirmations, and other methods to build confidence and to focus on thoughts that are likely to help, rather than hinder, game-day performance.

After lunch, Zinsser meets with a West Point graduate who's now a captain back from tours of Iraq and Afghanistan. The captain is teaching military science and working out like a madman. In a few months, he'll travel to a secret location to participate in what he vaguely describes as a "special mission selection." As we talk, it becomes clear he's attempting to join the army's Delta Force, a special operations unit so secretive that the army declines to officially acknowledge that it exists. (Given the secrecy and occasional threats to Special Forces operators, I have opted not to disclose this officer's name.)

As the captain prepares for the selection process, from which most soldiers wash out, he's using his own motivational sound track, which Zinsser produced.

Set to the song "Radioactive" by Imagine Dragons, it begins: "This is it, my chance to take a big step toward accomplishing my dream of being a Delta Force operator." It reinforces the soldier's self-identity as "a relentless workhorse who can accomplish anything. . . . The officer of choice for any task or job." It focuses on how he's going to manage his time to reach peak fitness in the months ahead, how he will improve his navigation skills, and eat right to get his body ready.

This captain listens to this sound track over and over, getting psyched for the selection process, imagining his body getting stronger and visualizing himself at the front of the Delta force recruits as they slog through training courses. "I'm trusting in the fact that I'm putting in the work, so I can stop worrying whether I've worked hard enough, and just go execute," he says.

2.

In the moments before a performance event, it can be extremely useful to dial down the excessive anxiety you're feeling as much as you can, the way Noa Kageyama teaches students at Juilliard to do before auditions. But to really make the most of the final moments before you perform, reducing anxiety isn't enough. You also want to build positive emotions, such as confidence, self-efficacy, and power, and sports psychologists have spent decades figuring out the best ways to do that.

The field's roots lie in a midwestern university lab. Coleman Griffith grew up in Iowa and played collegiate baseball before landing a job as a psychology professor at the University of Illinois. In 1925, he opened Research in Athletics Laboratory. He published books and papers, including the 1926 book *Psychology of Coaching,* which contains a primer on how coaches should help athletes get "keyed up" before games, such as talking to teams about opponents' unfair tactics, shaming them by personal abuse, inspiring them by recalling their past achievements, or bringing in alumni to fire them up.

Today Griffith is recalled as the father of sports psychology, but the path from his early studies to the work being done by modern practitioners such as Nate Zinsser isn't exactly linear. In the early 1930s, the University of Illinois pulled funding for Griffith's lab; as a result, Griffith's research ended, and he trained no graduate students to follow in his footsteps. Then, in 1936, the chewing gum magnate Philip Wrigley, who owned the Chicago Cubs, asked Griffith to deploy his psychological techniques on the baseball team.

Griffith recommended modifications to the team's practice regimen. (Example: Coaches should conduct infield practice at shorter distances to improve fielders' reaction times.) The team mostly ignored his suggestions. "The clash of cultures between the baseball players and the university professor seems to have been almost immediate," historian Christopher Green writes. The tension was particularly acute between Griffith and the team's manager (he dubbed Griffith "the headshrinker"), who Griffith felt was sabotaging and bad-mouthing his work. Few of Griffith's ideas were implemented, and his engagement with the Cubs lasted less than two years. Along with the demise of his research lab and his failure to train a next generation of researchers, Griffith's failure to help the Cubs is another reason sports psychology failed to take hold.

The field remained mostly dormant until the mid-1960s, and the discipline's first academic journal didn't come into existence until 1970. Since then, the field has progressed in fits and starts. (One of the fits: When the San Diego Chargers hired a team psychiatrist in 1973, he was caught prescribing steroids and amphetamines to players.) But by the 1980s, sports psychologists were regularly consulting with U.S. Olympic teams, and by the 1990s some Division I universities had psychologists working with varsity athletes.

Still, in many sports, even elite athletes remain completely unschooled in the techniques taught by Zinsser and his colleagues. In some cases, there remains a stigma about working with a psychologist. It somehow suggests weakness or mental illness. In team sports, some coaches consider the mental part of the game to be part of their purview, and they're reluctant to cede power to an outsider. Often athletes, parents, or schools lack the resources to provide sports psychologists. Even for those willing to pay, it can be hard to locate a qualified professional. In the United States, there are just 390 certified members of the Association for Applied Sports Psychologists, according to its online directory. As a result, sports psychology is a discipline with a powerful arsenal of tools of which a broad population of athletes remains largely ignorant.

3.

Nick Bollettieri is eighty-four years old and has been coaching tennis for more than sixty years. His roster of past pupils includes ten players who've been ranked number one in the world, including Andre Agassi, Boris Becker, Monica Seles, and Venus and Serena Williams. By all rights, Bollettieri should probably be retired and spending time with his current wife, his eighth.

Instead, he begins most mornings at 6 A.M. beside a tennis court in Bradenton, Florida, giving lessons for $900 per hour. The court is one of dozens on the campus of IMG Academy, a five-hundred-acre training center for elite athletes. Bollettieri founded the facility—a boarding school originally focused on tennis instruction—in 1978. Nine years later he sold it to IMG, the sports agency that has represented skier Lindsey Vonn and quarterback Peyton Manning, and IMG expanded it into new sports. Today IMG Academy has more than a thousand students who pay $72,000 per year to live at the school and train in sports ranging from golf and tennis to football and lacrosse.

For a sports fan, it's an incredible place to hang out. Wander by the tennis courts and watch a powerful young man—the world's number four ranked under-eighteen player—firing serves, while out on a driving range, last year's Women's U.S. Open champion crushes long irons under her coach's supervision. While IMG is best known for launching young prospects into professional sports careers, it also prepares athletes for collegiate competition: At a morning ceremony on the day I happened to visit, thirty-two IMG students signed commitment letters to attend colleges whose athletic programs had recruited them.

In addition to state-of-the-art advice on strength training and nutrition, IMG's students also benefit from a nine-person team dedicated to "mental coaching." A staff this size makes IMG a big player in the field; former members of its staff work for a variety of professional sports teams (particularly in baseball), and over the last decade it's trained dozens of psychologists who now work with the Navy SEALS and other military outfits.

Taking a break from a lesson on the tennis courts, Bollettieri argues that mental training has always been part of what good coaches do. He refers to a saying attributed to Vince Lombardi, an old friend of his: "We didn't lose the game. We just ran out of time." That shows the pervasive confidence and optimism the best athletes learn to adopt, he says. "You should judge a person by the effort they put into things, not the results," Bollettieri tells me. "What happens today is children are graded by the results they attain, which is wrong. . . . The scoreboard may say you lost based on the score, but if you did everything you could, you won."

Whether you learn these lessons from the psychologists at IMG, or in the PL360: Psychology of Elite Performance course at West Point, or by reading *Sports Psychology for Dummies,* or in a more sophisticated textbook (*Applied Sports Psychology* by Jean M. Williams is the one most pros recommended to me), the fundamentals are the same. Many of them aim to teach performers to increase their confidence and focus. To do it, the psychologists teach techniques including self-talk, mental rehearsal, and visualization.

We've all seen the crowd at NCAA basketball games waving and cheering behind the glass backboards to try to distract a free-throw shooter. Elite athletes are taught to tune out distracting, irrelevant stimuli and focus on the task at hand. Psychologists distinguish between attentional tasks that are narrow, such as a baseball hitter tracking a pitched ball, versus broad, such as a quarterback surveying the entire field before deciding where to pass. They also distinguish between external tasks, typically involving other players or game conditions, versus internal tasks, things that take place in your head. They can offer specific drills to increase athletes' ability to use these different types of focus and to retain their ability to concentrate even as the environment changes (say, at an away game with a hostile crowd) or the stakes around the performance grow higher.

There's a relationship between a free-throw shooter's ability to tune out distractions and confidence, because his focus is partly dependent on feeling assured he's going to make the shot. Indeed, research shows a direct link between confidence and performance, which is why so many star athletes come across as cocky. While sports psychologists don't seek to breed arrogance, they do systematically try to instill confidence by teaching athletes to remember successes and explain away failures.

Much of the psychological work to build confidence focuses on self-talk, the internal dialogue in our heads. Many people have a tendency to be self-critical, negative, or pessimistic, and sports psychologists seek to avert that behavior by teaching thought-blocking techniques or cues and affirmations to focus on before or during performances. At times, these techniques may feel a bit like the affirmations offered by Stuart Smalley, the *Saturday Night Live* character played by Al Franken in the 1990s. ("I'm good enough, smart enough, and doggone it, people like me.") But even if they feel a little silly, decades of research show that they work.

If positive self-talk is an audio sound track, mental imagery and visualization go further, involving all the senses, as an athlete imagines what a successful performance looks like in the moments before she begins. Elite golfers typically visualize every shot before they take it. Some will intentionally imagine a hole looking super-sized, to make the putt seem easier. In faster-moving sports or other venues, people visually rehearse important movements ahead of time. One sports psychologist told me how, at the 1988 Olympics, U.S. track athletes were offered the opportunity to visit the stadium for a walk-through the day before competition began. Most declined, preferring to nap at the hotel. But Edwin Moses meticulously toured the locker rooms, then set up hurdles around the track. He carefully took off his sweats, just as he would at a competition, and then walked around the track, over and over, visualizing how he hoped to perform.

At IMG Academy or elsewhere, the specifics of how students are taught these skills will vary from coach to coach; the process will also vary based on the sport they play. Self-talk is especially important in slower-moving sports like golf, in which players have lots of downtime between shots to think positive (or negative) thoughts. In team sports, training in self-talk and concentration may focus on the team dynamic, such as avoiding getting distracted or turning negative by comparing oneself with a teammate.

Many of the ideas in sports psychology echo the tenets of the positive psychology movement pioneered by University of Pennsylvania psychologist Martin Seligman in the 1990s. Aside from emphasizing qualities such as optimism and confidence, both positive psychology and performance psychology share an ethos that everyone can and should benefit from these "enhancement" techniques. That's in contrast to traditional clinical psychology, which is aimed at treating maladaptive or neurotic behaviors. This is one reason IMG avoids using variations of the word "psychology," and instead refers to "mental coaching" or "mental conditioning."

David Hesse, IMG's director of athletic and personal development, worked for a British management consulting firm before quitting to study sports psychology. From the time he spent inside corporations, he has no doubt the techniques being taught to world-class athletes in his offices work equally well outside of sports. "These tools apply to any type of high performance, whether you're in an emergency room, a law firm, a courtroom, a boardroom," he says. "We're biological creatures, and we have that fight-or-flight response, even in a corporate setting. These tools can absolutely help."

4.

If you happen to attend a conference at which Jonathan Jenkins is speaking, you'll probably notice how calm and confident he appears. It looks like he's given this same talk hundreds of times, even though today's topic is specific to this particular event, so he can't simply be repeating an old speech. The second thing you may notice is how, about five minutes into his talk, the speech seems to make an abrupt pivot.

Jenkins's introductory remarks are autobiographical, and at some events they don't seem particularly relevant to the topic listed on the agenda. He talks about his childhood in Texas, and how his original goal in life was to be a cowboy. (He'll often show a slide of himself as a child wearing a Lone Ranger mask.) He describes being hospitalized at age twelve, and how he read a book about China over and over as he recovered. That book led him to want to live in China, so after college he asked his parents for an airline ticket to Beijing. He lived there for several years, and during his time in China he wound up launching a company, now called OrderWithMe, that helps small companies compete with big-box retailers.

Only after he's related his personal story does he segue—sometimes smoothly, sometimes a little jarringly—into the specific message of that day's particular speech.

As a start-up CEO, presentations are crucial to Jenkins's job. He's pitched his company to dozens of venture capitalists, successfully raising millions of dollars in funding. He frequently gives keynotes to industry conferences. On average, Jenkins gives one speech a week. He considers anything fewer than a hundred people a "small group," and doesn't consider it a "big speech" unless the audience is more than a thousand.

Jenkins is also extremely busy. He has limited time to write speeches, and he doesn't have much time to rehearse. So he's developed a unique technique: For nearly every speech he gives, he uses a standard autobiographical introduction, a well-honed, memorized set of remarks he's used hundreds of times. As a result, Jenkins doesn't have to think about what he's saying during the first few moments of a speech. He needn't figure out when to pause for effect or an audience reaction. Like a trucker changing lanes or a nurse who's taking a temperature, he's doing something that he's already done so often it requires no active thought. He can go on autopilot, speaking without a hint of nerves before he segues into the custom-tailored portion of the speech. By that point, he's won over the crowd.

"I start with my story," Jenkins says. "I figure if I got invited to speak at an event, there's something in my background or past that prepared me to be there talking, so the first part of the speech is always trying to make a personal connection with the audience." The biographical opener sets the stage and lets him gain confidence on the stage telling a story he knows cold.

The standardized opening isn't Jenkins's only strength as a speaker. His grandfather was a Southern preacher, and by the time Jenkins was ten, his grandfather was routinely asking him to speak to the congregation, which usually numbered around two hundred people. While still in grade school, Jenkins learned to gauge and hold the audience's interest, and to treat public speaking as a fun opportunity to tell a story. By the time he left for college, he was completely comfortable being at a podium with hundreds of eyes staring at him.

Right about now you should be saying: "Hold up. You're talking about practice, not getting psyched up. Jonathan Jenkins gives great speeches because he's spent ten thousand hours doing it—not because of anything he does in the final few minutes before he performs."

I appreciate your skepticism. You're right, to a point. Jenkins *is* a practiced speaker, and his standard opening wouldn't work if he hadn't done it so often.

But his story still belongs in this book, because he's found a way to increase his confidence even when speaking to a thousand people, and even during the part of a speech in which most people are most nervous—the very beginning. He's turned what's ordinarily a cognitively demanding task into something he recite easily from memory.

The Nobel Laureate Daniel Kahneman describes human cognition as operating in two distinct modes, which he calls System 1 and System 2. "System 1 operates automatically and quickly, with little or no effort and no sense of voluntary control," Kahneman writes in *Thinking, Fast and Slow*. "System 2 allocates attention to the effortful mental activities that demand it."

For most people, making a high-stakes presentation is a

System 2 mental activity. But grafting something that's automatic onto the front end of every presentation, Jenkins has effectively turned the opening into a System 1 task.

Along with "relax" and "calm down," another piece of standard advice for people in a nervous-making situation is "Don't overthink it." This advice makes sense because there are many situations in which thinking too much (or operating in System 2) is only going to cause problems. In these contexts, it's better to find a way to shift to System 1, and to go on autopilot.

Sian Beilock has spent twenty years studying how, when, and why people cause problems by overthinking. It's a topic she learned about firsthand as a teenager. At fifteen, she was a soccer goalie in the U.S. Youth Soccer Olympic Development Program, a path that could have led her to Olympic or World Cup competition. Then one day, with the Olympic coach watching from just behind her goal, she could feel her brain behaving differently. "I felt self-conscious," she recalls. "I had a total meltdown and let in two goals." Her dreams of playing soccer in the Olympics ended that afternoon.

But in the insight that her brain seemed to function differently under pressure, she found the beginnings of her academic career. As an undergrad she studied cognitive science, then she went on to earn doctorates in psychology and exercise science at Michigan State. Later she moved to the University of Chicago, where much of her research utilized a putting green, tricky math tests, and MRI machines.

Early in her graduate work, Beilock became especially interested in two theories of why people choke under pressure, and how these forces exert themselves differently during different kinds of tasks. As she explained in her master's thesis, some believe that distraction is a primary culprit when people fail under pressure. Instead of applying their attention and focus to the task at hand, people see their concentration sapped away by so-called task-irrelevant cues. Others believe the real culprit is explicit monitoring, which describes the exact opposite phenomenon: You become so keenly aware and overfocused on what you're doing that you screw it up. The phrase "self-conscious" is aptly descriptive: You become *too* conscious of yourself.

Beilock has been particularly fascinated by how these two forces play out in "proceduralized" activities that people don't think about, and in activities that put demands on people's working memory. Someone who plays a ton of golf has likely proceduralized putting. They can do it on autopilot. For this person, overthinking a putt is bad. Complicated math, on the other hand, requires one's working memory, so overthinking is good and autopilot would be problematic.

As Beilock writes in her 2010 book *Choke:* "The key is to have brainpower at your disposal, but to be able to 'turn it off' in situations where it may prove disadvantageous." Choking, she writes, is usually the result of people "paying too much attention to what they are doing or not devoting enough brainpower to the task."

As Beilock's research makes clear, an important element when getting psyched up to perform is to decide whether this is the kind of task you should be thinking about, or whether you should be on autopilot. Or, to put it in Kahneman's language, should this activity utilize System 1 or System 2? Professional golfers should autopilot their putts; novice golfers, who haven't practiced a putt thousands of time, need to give each putt more thought.

Together, Jonathan Jenkins and Sian Beilock illustrate a part of psyching up that many people have never considered: In the moments before you perform, decide whether you'll do better with your brain turned on or off, and proceed accordingly.

5.

Listening to motivational sound tracks and repeating positive affirmations aren't the only ways to instill a sense of confidence before you perform. There are also ways to activate these emotions subconsciously, and research suggests it can be done by simply glancing at a photograph.

Consider, for example, the photo hanging on the wall of Gary Latham's office at the University of Toronto. It's a large poster of a pole-vaulter who's trying to clear a high bar. Underneath the image is a caption: "If at first you don't succeed . . ." A colleague gave Latham the poster twenty-five years ago when he became department chair. Latham put it up on the wall and forgot about it. He never considered the banal image might make him better at his job. However, over the last decade, he's done research suggesting this simple poster might help put him in the right mindset to perform.

Latham is an organizational psychologist who's spent more than forty years studying how people set conscious goals and go about achieving them. As Latham did his own research, a completely different set of studies made him angry—so angry that he set about trying to debunk them.

The research involved a concept called priming. John Bargh, the Yale psychology professor who's the field's best-known researcher, defines priming as the study of "the temporary activation state of an individual's mental representations, and how these internal readinesses interact with environmental information to produce perceptions, evaluations, and even motivations and social behavior."

That's a complicated explanation, but it becomes easy to understand if you read about experiments in the field. Many of them ask subjects to solve simple word puzzles that, through subtle word choices, attempt to subconsciously manipulate the subject's mental state, predisposing them to behave in a certain way. In a famous 1996 experiment, for instance, Bargh and some colleagues gave one set of subjects a word puzzle featuring words such as "rude," "impolite," and "obnoxious" (along with many other nonthematic words), and another set of subjects a puzzle featuring "cordially," "patiently," and "appreciate." (A third group was primed with neutral words.) Then they placed the subjects, one by one, in a scenario in which they awaited instructions from someone engaged in conversation with a third person, and measured how long each subject waited before interrupting the conversation. They found the people who'd been primed to be rude interrupted the conversation far more quickly than people who'd been primed to be polite or hadn't been primed at all.

In the same study, Bargh primed a group of subjects with words like "Florida," "wrinkle," and "ancient," and then measured how long each person took to walk down a hallway when leaving the experiment, compared to control groups. The result: being primed with words that connote "elderly" makes people walk more slowly, as if they were elderly, too.

As Latham read Bargh's studies, he recalls thinking they were "unadulterated bullshit." Latham believes the conscious mind guides behavior, and that all this subconscious mumbo jumbo was as suspect as the fraudulent 1950s experiment in which moviegoers allegedly bought more popcorn and soda after split-second subliminal ads for those products were inserted into a film. (The movie-snack experiment was later found to be a hoax.) Latham's disapproval notwithstanding, by the early 2000s the priming studies were catching on. Bargh won wide professional acclaim, and

Latham saw an influx of young grad students who were convinced of the power of priming. So he cooked up a plan to prove that priming is just plain nonsense.

Unlike previous researchers, who did their experiments in labs, Latham decided to look for evidence of priming in an actual workplace: a university call center, where workers telephone alumni to solicit donations. His research team gave eighty-one employees an information packet outlining the day's calls, but some of the packets were different from the others. One set contained an inspirational photo of a runner crossing a finish line. The study was designed to find out if just glimpsing a photo denoting success would affect how well the telemarketers performed. Can this simple image subconsciously prime workers to do their jobs better?

The results were unmistakable: Workers whose packets contained the photo raised significantly more money than the unprimed workers. When Latham saw the results, "I nearly fell off of my chair," he says. The whole point of the study was to *disprove* that priming really works. Latham assumed he'd made an error, so he began visiting other call centers to do similar studies. Each time, the results showed that workers whose instructions contained the photo raised more money. "I reluctantly shifted from being skeptical to being a believer," Latham says.

In subsequent papers, Latham expanded on those findings. In one study, also in a fund-raising call center, he tested how workers who viewed the same finish line photo performed against people primed with a "context-specific" photo—in this case, happy workers wearing telephone headsets in a customer service setting. His team found that call center workers who'd viewed the motivational call center photo performed better than people viewing the running photo (and better than the control group), and that the effect lasted not only for a few hours, but for several days. In another study, he tested how well fifty teams performed in a group activity in which they were asked to prioritize a list of survival items they'd need if they were in a spaceship that crash-landed on the moon. (This is a standard academic exercise to judge how well teams function.) Sure enough, the groups whose instructions had included a photo of a small team of people cooperatively working on a task around a table did better on the task, as measured by how closely their picks mirrored a team of NASA experts' choices.

Latham isn't the only one exploring how priming can be a tool in workplace scenarios.

The best-known research that marries priming with the type of work done by white-collar workers has been done by Amy Cuddy of Harvard Business School. In 2010, Cuddy and some colleagues published a paper describing how they'd asked forty-two people to position their body in either a "high-power" or "low-power" pose, then engage in a risk-taking task, with each subject giving a saliva sample before and after the exercise. The "high-power" pose required standing with their hands on hips and feet apart, like Wonder Woman, or if seated, with their hands interlocked behind their heads, their feet up on a desk, their body open and exposed. The before and after spit tests showed that people who'd positioned themselves in the "high-power" pose experienced a marked increase in testosterone—a hormone associated with aggression—and a decrease in cortisol—a hormone marking stress. People who'd used "low-power" poses, with their arms crossed and their body contracted and small, experienced the opposite hormonal reactions. When it came to the risk-taking task, people who'd spent time in the power pose were much more willing to take risks. "The high-power posers reported feeling significantly more 'powerful' and 'in charge,'" the study said. "A simple two-minute power-pose manipulation was enough to significantly alter the physiological, mental, and feeling states of our participants."

Cuddy's 2012 TED Talk on the research went viral, and was followed by her 2015 book *Presence*. The work has turned her into a star, but it's also proven controversial. Several other sets of researchers failed to find the same effect when they replicated the original experiment, and various statisticians have raised doubts about how the methodology and number crunching may have led to a "spurious" conclusion. In 2016, one of Cuddy's collaborators on the original 2010 paper disavowed the results. In response, Cuddy said that despite the conflicting studies, at least nine other experimenters had found support for the basic gist behind what she describes as the "power-posing effect"—specifically, that "adopting expansive poses can make people feel more powerful." Despite the scientific doubts, Cuddy's work remains popular because it offers a seductive hook. "If you tweak your posture just a little bit, it could significantly change the way your life unfolds," she says.

Columbia professor Adam Galinsky and his colleagues have done research that offers a quieter, more private method to achieve the same end. In a 2013 paper, they asked people to write about a time they felt powerful or powerless for a few minutes, before compiling a job application letter or taking part in a mock interview. In both experiments, the people who wrote about a time when they felt powerful performed better. In an interview, Galinsky argued that, for most people, writing about their own power will be more effective than power posing. "Some people feel really inauthentic doing the posture," he says. "The recall task is more private. It allows you to think about what you experienced and felt in that situation, and I think it's easier to get into the right mindset."

It's important to note that in all these priming experiments, the subjects weren't aware of *why* they were posing like Wonder Woman, looking at photos of runners, or writing about a time when they felt powerful. This raises a crucial question: Since priming involves the subconscious mind, can people who purposefully power pose before an important event elicit the same thing intentionally?

In other words, can someone intentionally prime themselves? Or is priming more like tickling, which doesn't really work when you do it to yourself?

Some researchers are dubious about self-priming. "The quick answer is that priming is a passive effect, and knowing about it gets in the way," says Bargh, the Yale professor. However, he allows that if a person *wants* to be primed—for instance, if someone is on a diet and hopes to eat fewer calories—then priming that suggests healthy eating may create some effect, because the person's mind is already inclined toward that goal.

"My guess is the most practical self-priming in the conscious route would be for 'reminders' of what you want to attain—photographs of role models, or Post-it notes from one's spouse, or of your elementary-school child's drawings on the wall," Bargh says. "If they remind you of what you yourself want, then you won't fight the influence."

Latham, the Toronto professor, offers a similarly nuanced answer. Because priming, by definition, requires people to be unaware it is happening, self-priming is oxymoronic. "It's a contradiction in terms to say I'm going to self-prime but I'll be unaware I'm doing it," he says. Someone who power poses before giving a TED Talk isn't really priming. They're really engaged in a physical, ritualistic form of psyching up, Latham says.

However, he points to the pole-vaulter poster on his office wall as an example of the blurry line regarding awareness. He put the poster up decades ago, so it's something he did to himself. But he's seen it there every day for a quarter century, so he's not very conscious that it's hanging there. He never stops to focus on it or contemplate its meaning—it just blends into the background. At this point, if the image is exerting any influence on him, it's so subtle as to border on unconscious. "It's just on the wall and I'm not noticing it, so that could be an example of self-priming," he says.

Although Latham had never heard of it before I interviewed him, there's a company called Successories that's spent more than thirty years trying to capitalize on that concept. Based in a small office park just off Interstate 95 in Delray Beach, Florida, the company sells posters featuring words like "Discipline," "Accountability," "Strength," and "Persistence." Each boldface word is paired with inspirational quotations and artsy images. Its best-selling work of motivational art, which has brought in millions of dollars in revenue, features a photo of the University of Virginia crew team rowing on a river at sunset above the block letters "TEAM-WORK" and a quote from Andrew Carnegie about "the ability to work together toward a common vision."

Successories fills a basic need. Companies have blank office walls to fill. Managers can put up generic van Gogh reproductions, hang images specific to their business (glamour shots of products, for instance, or portraits of past CEOs), or hang posters that reinforce corporate virtues. Successories caters to the third category. "Our customers are putting something on the wall that can be deemed art, but it can be useful," says Eric Haber, Successories' president. "It's a passive billboard in the hallway. It says 'We believe in teamwork.' Nobody is actively saying it, but the art that exists in the common areas is saying it." Haber and his team routinely encounter Successories posters in car dealerships and high schools; one employee spotted one in the jury deliberation room at a courthouse.

Latham hasn't hung any new posters on his wall since the research turned him into a priming believer. But he has purchased a poster of *The Little Engine That Could* to adorn one of his grandchildren's walls. He hopes that every time his grandchild sees the message "I think I can, I think I can," he'll be primed with a message of self-efficacy and persistence.

While talking with Latham, I mention that a few years ago, while working as a magazine writer, I'd had a private office with a lot of blank walls. One day I'd thumbtacked up the cover of an issue for which I'd written the cover story. A few days later, our thoughtful office manager put it in a cheap frame, and the next time I wrote a cover story, she framed it and hung it up, too. Over the next few years the wall came to contain images of the dozen or so cover stories I'd written. While I didn't really notice them, they probably helped me feel more confident; as I struggled to write a new story, I could glance up at all the successful articles I'd written in the past. Subconsciously, those images probably prodded my mind to say: "I think I can." I told Latham about the wall adornments, and how, when I'd left that old job and moved to a new office, I'd left them sitting in a box, never bothering to locate a hammer or rehang them.

"This research is still at the embryonic stage," Latham cautions. "But I'd encourage you to hang them up."

Chapter Six

HARNESSING ANGER AND RIVALRY

*CAN FOCUSING ON COMPETITORS
MAKE US STRONGER?*

I t sounds like a scene from *Friday Night Lights*. It actually took place on a Thursday afternoon in 1988, in a high school gymnasium in northwest New Jersey.

At a podium near center court, the four cocaptains of the Warren Hills Regional High School football team took turns talking into a microphone, as eight hundred students listen politely from the bleachers. The following evening, these players would represent Warren Hills in the annual matchup against its archrival, the Hackettstown Tigers. So this afternoon, students were excused from classes for a pep rally. The marching band played. Cheerleaders did handsprings. And the team's captains talked about the importance of the game.

Hackettstown and Warren Hills are located nine miles apart

and have been playing each other since the 1930s, but this year was special. The Warren Hills team, on which I was a benchwarmer offensive lineman, was going into the game undefeated, at 6-0. Beating Hackettstown would give Warren Hill good odds of achieving an undefeated regular season and making the state playoffs. But even without that context, this is a rivalry that always mattered. "You could have a season where you lost every other game, but if you beat Hackettstown, you could still be happy," Andy Bordick, the team's center, recalled years later.

In the middle of the captains' pep talk, one of the gym doors opened loudly, interrupting the rally. A middle-aged man carrying a large white box walked straight to the center of the gymnasium, stopping in front of the principal. The football captains stopped speaking and watched, perplexed. Warren Hills is located in a town of only six thousand people, so many of the students recognized the man: He owned the local flower shop and had a son on the football team. The florist and the principal had a whispered conversation. The principal opened an envelope attached to the box, and then they motioned over the head football coach. The coach looked at the card and scowled. Then he carried the box to the podium.

"Boys, we have a special delivery," the coach said into the microphone, handing the box to his captains. One of them read the card aloud into the microphone:

To the Warren Hills Football Team

Please accept our condolences on your upcoming loss.

We can't wait to see you on Friday night.

Sincerely, the Hackettstown Tigers

Inside the box was a large bundle of carnations—blue and white, the Warren Hills team colors. Several weeks ago, these flowers were fresh and beautiful. By the time they were opened in the school gymnasium, however, they were rotting and putrid.

As the bleachers erupted in cries of dismay, one of the players threw a handful of carnations on the gym floor and began stomping them, like one of those cheesy, scripted scenes from a professional wrestling match. The coach grabbed the microphone and urged calm. The cheerleaders began a new cheer. And in the hours leading up to game time, the players seethed.

On the bus ride to the Friday night game, the players' anger was palpable. One lineman brought the dead carnations onto the bus, and then placed them on the field during warm-ups. Years later, the players recalled how the dead flower insult increased the level of hostility we felt, even for an opponent we already hated. And in this case, that emotion seemed to be productive: Led by our quarterback's strong arm and our stingy defense, Warren Hills won the game, 21-6, and went on to have their most successful season in years.

The dead flower delivery was one of those high school stories we remembered vividly. It was only years later, as we grew older, that we realized the Hackettstown team hadn't sent us the flowers. In fact, our own coaches had orchestrated the delivery. This epic act of disrespect was actually a self-inflicted psychological ploy. Our coaches wanted to make us angry, because everyone knows you perform better when you're filled with fury and resentment.

Right?

2.

During the 2016 Summer Olympics, the swimmer Michael Phelps was photographed moments before a race scowling intently at a South African opponent. Wearing headphones and a hood, Phelps's face is pointed down in the photo. His eyebrows jut out over his eyes. His lips are jammed together so tightly that they create a series of frowny dimples. Some commentators said the visage reminded them of a dog who's about to attack. The expression became known as #Phelpsface, and it quickly went viral. After the Olympics ended, the late-night host Jimmy Fallon invited Phelps on his show to teach him how he makes the expression.

Compare Phelps's pre-performance anger with that of Bob Cousy, the legendary Celtics guard. While preparing for the final game of the 1963 NBA championship, Bob Cousy spent thirty-six hours alone in a Los Angeles hotel room. He ordered all his meals from room service. He didn't answer the telephone. This would be the final game of Cousy's career, and he spent most of these solitary hours meditating on his hatred for Frank Selvy, the Laker guard he'd be covering in the game.

"If [Selvy] had walked into that room I might have leaped at his throat and tried to strangle him," Cousy recalled in his memoir. "If anyone had tried to touch me or even talked to me, I might have killed him, too." For Cousy, preparing for an important game meant orchestrating a feeling of controlled rage for his opponent, a skill he recalls as "my most important asset as a competitor." Cousy called it his "killer instinct." Even in regular season games that weren't particularly high stakes, Cousy would get angry before the games, and then hope an opposing player did something during the game—such as a dirty foul—to make him irate. "I played better when I was angry," he wrote. For Cousy, fomenting that anger was a key part of getting psyched up.

Is there actual science to show that people perform better when angry? In fact, there's very little, and the results aren't very conclusive. The evidence suggests it depends on the person and the sport. "'Old school' or traditional approaches to coaching have often relied on the belief that getting athletes angry will enhance arousal, energy and motivation," writes Paul A. Davis, one of the leading researchers into how anger affects athletes. Newer coaching strategies recognize it's important for players to be able to stay in control of their emotions, lest they suffer penalties or ejections due to an angry outburst. Experimental research suggests getting angry prior to powerlifting or playing other explosive sports (such as football or boxing) can increase one's strength and performance, but anger is likely to be detrimental in sports requiring fine motor skills, such as golf.

Outside of sports, the evidence is mixed, as well. Consider the practice of negotiation. Some people believe anger makes one seem more powerful or can scare an opponent, and therefore negotiating while angry will result in better outcomes. But research by Keith Allred, a former professor at Harvard's Kennedy School of Government, shows that anger often harms a negotiation by "escalating conflict, biasing perceptions, and making impasses more difficult," along with decreasing cooperation and raising the rate at which offers are rejected, according to an article in *Harvard Business Review*. The article concludes: "Bringing anger to a negotiation is like throwing a bomb into the process."

But simply thinking about "being angry" is too simple a construction. Psychologists think of emotions as manifesting in two ways: We can experience them, and we can express them. Experiencing an emotion is feeling it; no one else need know about it. When Bob Cousy is storming around his hotel room alone, he's feeling angry, but since no one else sees his behavior, he's not really expressing it. Expressing anger means making others aware of it, through words, facial expressions, or other actions. When Michael Phelps makes the #Phelpsface directly at an opponent, he's very clearly expressing anger, whether or not he's actually feeling it himself.

There's a third and related, but slightly different, set of feelings that performers can harness, too. Even before the Warren Hills football team opened up the rotting flowers, we were focused on a specific opponent. The players didn't start out angry—that came after the putrid flowers arrived—but we were thinking about our upcoming performance in a very specific context. We weren't just focused on "doing our best" in isolation, the way we might if we were running a race alone for time. By focusing on an opponent, we were framing our performance as a rivalry.

That, it turns out, is another force that can affect the way we perform.

3.

Whether or not feeling anger can boost performance, there's widespread belief that expressing anger at an opponent can throw him off his game. That's why trash talk has become an integral part of modern sports culture. In sports like boxing, it's an essential part of the way performers prepare before competing.

In the United States, professional basketball is the sport most associated with the practice. In one infamous 2013 incident, Kevin Garnett, a notorious smack-talker, baited opponent Carmelo Anthony by quietly telling him his wife "tastes like Honey Nut Cheerios," leading Anthony to go berserk on the court. Though it goes by different names, trash talk is a global phenomenon. In cricket, they call it "sledging," and the typical insults involve mocking a player's cricket skills or, like Garnett, suggesting carnal knowledge of an opponent's wife. "How's your wife and my kids?" goes one familiar line.

Once, trash talk was limited to pregame and during-game, but social media has caused it to spread. Today athletes can trash-talk at each other 24/7 on Twitter.

The greatest trash-talker of all-time broadcast his rhythmic put-downs in a time before Twitter wars, however. In his memoir, Muhammad Ali describes how, very early in his career, he was booked onto a radio show with Gorgeous George, the flamboyant professional wrestler. When the radio host asked George about his upcoming fight, he replied. "I'll kill him; I'll tear his arms off. If this bum beats me, I'll crawl across the ring and cut off my hair, but that's not going to happen, because I'm the greatest wrestler in the world!" Ali went to the wrestling match that night and saw a packed house. George's over-the-top rhetoric, Ali realized, drove fan interest and helped the bottom line. Ali recalled. "That's when I really started shouting 'I'm beautiful. I'm the greatest. I can't be beat, I'm the fastest thing on two feet, and I float like a butterfly and sting like a bee."

At times, Ali wasn't just showboating for the fans. He was clearly trying to intimidate opponents. Before his first fight with Sonny Liston, in 1964, Ali made a careful plan to shout at and attempt to scuffle with Liston at the prefight weigh-in. "I rehearsed and planned every move," Ali wrote later. "This is it, you big ugly bear," Ali screamed at his rival as he stepped toward the medical scale. "You'll be mine tomorrow night. . . . You're not The Champ— you're The Chump." Ali lunges at Liston, ready to scuffle—a move he'd choreographed in advance with his handlers, who held him back. If you watch the clip even fifty years later, you'll instantly recognize Liston's expression. He looks scared.

The rhyming insults, the boasting, and the predictions about the round in which he'd knock out opponents continued, and they're part of what made Ali such a charismatic figure. "He entertained as much with his mouth as with his fists, narrating his life with a patter of inventive doggerel," wrote Robert Lipsyte in Ali's 2016 obituary.

Few of us would have the ability to denigrate opponents as cleverly as Ali. But it's worth asking: If we choose to give it a shot, will it help us perform better, or intimidate opponents into performing worse?

Ben Conmy grew up in England, where his father was a

professional soccer player. The younger Conmy played soccer, too, and as the level of competition increased in his late teens, so did the level of trash talk. "The higher I went, the talk became much more pointed, more focused, vicious, and cruel—psychotic stuff, really, coming from sixteen, seventeen, and eighteen-year-old kids," he says. Conmy had a tendency to respond verbally to trash talk, and sometimes it would make him play worse. His father routinely chided him to cut it out. "Completely ignore them. All it's going to do is detract from you playing well," his dad would say. Conmy couldn't help himself. "To me, trash talk almost became a game within the game, and I was always fascinated with it."

By the early 2000s, Conmy was pursuing a doctorate in sports psychology at Florida State University, and he wanted to focus his studies on trash talk. His academic advisers were against it. There was hardly any academic literature on the practice. "We don't know how you'll do a literature review, and how are you going to study this?" they said. Conmy was resolute. "To me, trash talk is just a fundamental part of sports, and it can impact a win or a loss," he says, insisting it was worthy of study.

To placate him, his advisers allowed him to convene four small focus groups—two sets of eight female athletes and two sets of eight males—as a pilot study, to try to determine if this was important enough for a dissertation. In the focus groups, the athletes talked about their experiences giving and receiving trash talk. One athlete stood out. "There was this angelic-looking, lovely female lacrosse player," Conmy recalls. She described how, before every game, she ran past the line of opposing players, screaming as loudly as possible: *"I'm going to shove this stick up your ass."* "She'd yell things about their family," Conmy says. "She wanted people to think she was completely psychotic before the game even began, and then she'd continue it throughout the competition." Conmy had the focus groups transcribed, and showed the results to his professors. "They couldn't believe the things she said," he recalls. "They said 'Okay, go ahead and research this.'"

In the resulting thesis, Conmy argues that trash talk is as old as the Bible. When David boasted to Goliath before their fight that "I will strike you down and cut off your head," he was talking smack. Conmy defines the practice as "the deliberate act of verbal communication aimed at gaining a tangible advantage (psychological or physical) over an opponent," and describes a conceptual framework in which trash talk affects performance by disrupting a rival player's cognitive and affective states, interfering with perceived self-efficacy and perceived performance.

Conmy then surveyed 274 college athletes about their experiences with trash talk. The numbers demonstrated widely held belief in its effectiveness. Nearly 90 percent believe it directly affected an athlete's performance, and three quarters said it could affect athletes' belief in themselves. More than three quarters also said that trash talk "always" or "almost always" was evident in their sports, which ranged from basketball and football to track and swimming.

The data suggests that athletes see some opponents as especially susceptible to trash talk, while more confident and focused athletes remain relatively unaffected. All else equal, witty and clever trash talk is more effective, as is talk that's repeated frequently. Although the athletes generally believed in the effectiveness of trash talk, they also believe it can backfire: More than 80 percent recalled an instance when trash talk directed at them inspired them to perform better.

For his dissertation, Conmy followed up the survey work with a controlled experiment in which forty men played a *Madden NFL* video game, in which some were allowed to trash-talk while some stayed silent. Those results showed most players prefer to trash-talk because they find it motivational, and although players didn't actually perform better while trash-talking they did show increases in self-efficacy and positive affect.

Conmy's work jibes with what little other academic work exists on the subject. For instance, a 2010 study by David W. Rainey and Vincent Granito of 414 college athletes found that males trash-talk more than females, that Division I athletes do it more than Division III athletes, and that the goals are the same: to motivate themselves and to destabilize opponents. Some of Rainey's results are surprising. Respondents said they first used trash talk, on average, at age eleven. Ten percent said that trash talk often denigrates a rival's family, and 7 percent admitted to using racial insults. Among female athletes, trash talk often focuses on appearance, with two insults predominating: "You're fat" and "You're ugly."

After Conmy finished his dissertation, he left academics; he now works with athletes as a sports psychologist. Trash talk often comes up in his work as a challenge facing his clients. But he says that as he's grown older, he's become aware of how much the practice transcends sports. Some of the most ardent trash-talkers he knows are friends who work in banking in London. "They seek out the pub of rival hedge fund guys, and they go in there specifically to talk shit at the top of their voices about how well their portfolios are doing," he says. He points to the character of Ari Gold on HBO's *Entourage* series as another businessperson who's constantly putting down others as a way to enhance his own performance.

"Quite a lot of businesspeople are frustrated athletes, or they were very good athletes when they were younger," he says. "They saw how trash talk worked in athletics, and if it worked in athletics, why wouldn't it work in another competitive environment?"

4.

In the 1890s, bicycling became a popular American pastime, and among the enthusiasts was an Indiana University graduate student named Norman Triplett. Triplett liked sports of all kinds: He ran (and later coached) track, and played on an adult baseball team. But his observations of the behavior of bicyclists led him to conduct a set of experiments for which he's remembered even today.

Analyzing data from a set of 1897 bicycle races, Triplett observed how the riders' speeds varied as they raced in one of three conditions: unpaced competition (a single rider striving individually to achieve the fastest time), a paced competition (in which the single rider is assisted by a team that rides ahead at a prescribed pace), and an actual race, in which riders are cycling in real time against one another.

As Triplett analyzed data from over two thousand riders, he noticed that riders following a pacemaker rode at speeds averaging 34.4 seconds faster per mile than unpaced riders. Moreover, riders who competed alongside one another rode nearly forty seconds faster per mile than unpaced riders. Triplett hypothesized several reasons for the faster speeds, including a "suction" or "shelter" theory (in which riders achieve a mechanical advantage by drafting behind the other riders), as well as various psychological theories. For instance, he suggested riders may be hypnotized or put into an autopilot mode by the presence of competitors.

Triplett eventually concluded there's another force at work, one he called dynamogenic factors. "This theory of competition holds that the bodily presence of another rider is a stimulus to the racer in arousing the competitive instinct," he wrote, with the other rider providing "an inspiration to greater effort."

To test this theory, Triplett devised a competition involving a contraption that resembled two side-by-side fishing reels, and used forty schoolchildren as subjects who competed in reeling contests, against each other and against the clock. The result: The head-to-head reelers consistently performed better. Triplett concluded: "[Having] another contestant participating simultaneously in the race serves to liberate latent energy not ordinarily available."

In other words, we try harder when we're competing directly against another competitor. And while Triplett's study doesn't directly address the best way to prepare for such competitions, it makes sense that thinking about the opponent and your desire to beat him *before* you begin pedaling would increase motivation and energy, too.

Triplett's conclusion isn't very surprising to anyone who's played a sport. "Competition spurs motivation, one way or another—whether it's because a competitor wants to win or because a competitor simply doesn't want to come out on the bottom," write Po Bronson and Ashley Merryman in *Top Dog: The Science of Winning and Losing*. "Even when we are dragged into competitions we'd rather not be in, the fact we are being compared to others triggers our competitive instincts and we try harder." Bronson and Merryman point out that the phenomenon isn't limited to athletics. "Some of the greatest teams in history were equally well known for the hostility among the collaborators," they write, citing Abraham Lincoln's "Team of Rivals," the scientists leading the Manhattan Project, and the Mercury astronauts.

For many years, managers have tried to harness the power of competition within workplaces. Particularly in the sales function, managers use leaderboards (which tell everyone who's selling more or less) and contests (often featuring trips or other prizes) to use people's natural drive to beat others and turn it into revenue. Lately, managers outside the sales function have used "gamification" to utilize the motivational power of competition. Some universities rely on "forced curve" grading systems, which limit how many students can get As and create a built-in zero-sum competitive dynamic in classroom performance. Companies also use forced-curve performance evaluation systems, in which only so many employees can get a top rating. This dynamic isn't limited to our work lives. If you wear a Fitbit and compare how many steps you're walking against your friends, you're gamifying fitness and trying to turn rivalry into a performance enhancer.

Rivalry is related to, but slightly different from, pure competition. While we can compete against anyone (even strangers), rivals are *specific* opponents with whom we feel an enhanced or special sense of competition. The Yankees and Red Sox qualify as rivals, as do Harvard and Yale. Rivalries are common in business, too: witness Coke and Pepsi, or CVS and Walgreens. And if Norman Triplett is remembered as the psychologist who first proved that competition can help people perform better, a modern-day New York University psychologist named Gavin Kilduff is working to prove that the special kind of competition experienced by rivals can boost performance even more.

It's a dynamic that Kilduff first discovered as a child, when he played video games and basketball with friends. Instead of just playing for fun, he constantly tried to increase the competitive dynamic by creating tournaments. He found that he always tried a little harder when competing against his closest friends.

In his research, Kilduff has explored the factors that drive rivalry, and how it can impact performance. In one study, he found that rivalries are driven by similarities between opponents, the frequency with which they compete, and how evenly matched they are. In a study of NCAA basketball teams, for instance, Kilduff found that teams play more efficient defense and block more shots when competing against a rival. In another study that asked people to think back on their own performance, he found that people recalled being more motivated and performing better when competing against a rival; more important than the self-reported results are actual race results featuring long-distance runners, in which competitors facing off against rivals did, in fact, run faster.

Kilduff says that rivalry often features a sense of hostility or animosity, but this isn't always the case. "One doesn't have to come with the other," Kilduff says, citing Larry Bird and Magic Johnson as intense rivals who had a cordial friendship off the court.

In sports, most rivalries evolve organically over time. But when a coach or leader is trying to psych up his team and no natural rivalry exists, there's an obvious strategy to attempt to utilize the positive effects of this dynamic: You create one.

5.

John Legere works from a relatively modest corner office on the top floor of a building in the Seattle suburb of Bellevue, Washington. His desk sits diagonally across the room, and behind it on a credenza rests a computer screen so gigantic at first I mistook it for a big-screen television. Legere, who is fifty-eight but looks younger, has longish dark hair combed straight back, reaching down his neck. On his left hand he wears a gigantic Batman ring. His attire pushes the extreme boundaries of "business casual": On the afternoon I meet with him, he's wearing a black and magenta tracksuit over a magenta T-shirt, magenta socks, and custom-made black-and-magenta sneakers. Black and magenta, it turns out, are the corporate colors of T-Mobile. Legere, who is T-Mobile's CEO, dresses this way every day.

Legere arrived at T-Mobile after a long career at AT&T and Global Crossing, companies where he usually wore a suit and tie. His stint as CEO of the latter company made him rich, and when he left Global Crossing after a 2011 merger, he didn't really need to work again. But by 2012 he was bored, so when a recruiter called to talk to him about becoming the CEO of T-Mobile, he was intrigued. T-Mobile was owned by a German telecom giant who'd tried to sell it to AT&T, but the Federal Trade Commission blocked the deal. Morale at T-Mobile was horrible. It was then the smallest of the four substantial U.S. wireless carriers and they were struggling. "Employees were beaten down," says Legere, recalling his first day. But he saw a bright side. "The average age of employees was twenty-seven, and they were pretty easy to wind up," he says. "They just needed to be told everything was going to be okay."

To fix the business, Legere made some basic moves, including inking a deal with Apple to sell the iPhone and taking steps to improve T-Mobile's poor cellular coverage, long an Achilles' heel. He led an IPO, to reduce financial reliance on the German parent company. He took steps to try to improve the culture, such as immediately rescinding a policy that retail employees could not have tattoos or facial piercings. But his larger strategy involved relentlessly targeting and calling out his rivals, and to use these constant put-downs of competitors as a way to psych up his own workforce.

Within months of his arrival, he began incessantly taunting T-Mobile's primary competitors, Verizon and AT&T, as "dumb and dumber." He publicly called them "pricks." In his first press conference as CEO, he said, "I've seen more honesty in Match.com ads than I've seen in AT&T's coverage maps." In a Super Bowl advertisement, he ridiculed Verizon's claim of providing faster data service. In 2013 he joined Twitter, and in less than three years he tweeted more than 17,500 times. Many of his tweets feature him trashing his telecom rivals. By 2016 he had more than three million followers, a fan base so deep that Twitter created an emoji using the image of Legere's face—an honor previously reserved only for Pope Francis. Fast Company has called Legere the "profanity-spewing shock jock of Corporate America" and said that with his unusual dress and hairstyle, he looks more like a member of the rock band Kiss than a telecom exec.

The T-Mobile chief's penchant for trash-talking corporate rivals is unusual. At many large companies, executives are loath to even speak the name of the firms they compete against. These leaders look at business as a one-person, against-the-clock-style race; in this scenario, the motivational rhetoric is about simply doing your best instead of beating someone else.

Legere attributes his different mentality to his athletic background. "I grew up as a competitive runner, and I like rivalries. It's just part of who I am," he says. (He has run the Boston Marathon more than a dozen times.) "I like winning, but I enjoy it even more when I'm making someone else lose." He describes a key part of his early strategy at T-Mobile as "picking a villain," which in this case was AT&T. "AT&T had so dramatically screwed people on their first iPhone experience. There was just this pent-up hatred," he says. Legere recalls that anytime he was talking to a large group, he could simply ask, "How many people have AT&T as your wireless carrier?" followed by "Now how many of you hate them?" The room would be filled with raised hands.

T-Mobile is playing in an industry in which a rivalry strategy is likely to pay dividends. By now, just about every American adult has a mobile phone, so the industry's growth rate has stalled. For an individual firm to grow in a saturated market, it has to steal share from competitors. Legere says the strategy also makes sense because dissatisfaction with wireless providers tends to run high, due to what he calls the industry's "pain points"—the punitive long-term contracts, the opaque and mysterious extra fees for data or roaming, activities over which customers seem to have little control. In response, Legere's strategy hasn't just focused on calling out rivals, but on attacking the standard industry practices that the dominant players have institutionalized.

Legere also attributes his fondness for trash-talking, particularly on Twitter, to the fact that even as CEO of a $32 billion company, he has time on his hands. "I'm divorced, and both my daughters are older now," he says. "I live alone. I have no dog. So this is what I do." When he's having a drink alone in a bar, he says, he likes to challenge strangers to speed contests, in which each logs his smartphone into a particular Web site to find out who has the fastest upload and download speeds. (He says his T-Mobile phone always comes out on top.) When he wakes up in the middle of the night, he grabs his phone and begins answering tweets from customers. Listening to Legere describe his lifestyle, one almost begins to feel sorry for him—until you remember that he lives in an $18 million Central Park West penthouse once owned by William Randolph Hearst, where his current neighbor is Giorgio Armani.

Much of Legere's trash-talking is aimed at consumers, to try to educate them to T-Mobile's competitive strengths against Verizon and AT&T. But there's a second audience for this bravado: his employees. "When I go after the other guys, they love it," Legere says, describing his frequent visits to customer call centers, where the headphone-wearing reps greet him like a rock star. Motivating low-paid employees to slog it out in a call center isn't easy, but when the reps can witness the CEO giving out his personal e-mail address and trashing T-Mobile's rivals on Twitter each day, it provides a morale boost. It makes them feel a sense of purpose about heading into a difficult job every morning.

Some of Legere's stunts seem ridiculously over the top. On at least one occasion, he's hired skywriting planes to scrawl putdowns in the air above AT&T's headquarters. The week before I met with him, Legere had bid $21,800 on eBay for the right to put a 9-square-inch temporary tattoo on the shoulder of U.S. Olympic runner Nick Symmonds during the 2016 Summer Games. For Legere, the obvious move would be to put the T-Mobile logo on Symmonds's arm. But on the day we met, Legere said he was contemplating a different plan, one suggested by his Twitter followers: that instead of promoting T-Mobile, Symmonds's tattoo should simply read "F—k AT&T."

As it tweaks rivals, it helps that T-Mobile is a smaller player attacking larger companies. Anyone who follows sports has witnessed the inherent appeal of underdog narratives—the way we reflexively support an unlikely team with a so-called Cinderella story. Academic research suggests this dynamic plays out in business, as well. Georgetown professor Neeru Paharia and colleagues have studied why and how consumers respond to businesses that position themselves as underdogs. In one experiment that involved giving coupons to bookstore patrons, for instance, they found consumers who were alerted to the fact that the small bookstore's primary rivals were "large, multibillion-dollar corporations" purchased more than shoppers given neutral positioning statements. Beyond rooting for smaller, independent brands, consumers "may want to punish stronger competitors, enjoy watching them fail, and gain pleasure as they 'stick it to the man,'" the researchers write. "In the context of competition, in addition to supporting underdogs, consumers may also want to punish larger, more dominant brands for having too much power."

Across Lake Washington, in downtown Seattle, lies a company that started out as an underdog but is now dominant in its field: Amazon. In 2014, when I interviewed founder Jeff Bezos, I asked him about the merits of focusing on rivals as a motivating force. "There are companies out there where they wake up in the morning, and they organize their internal thoughts by who the competition is, and how they're going to beat the competition," Bezos told me. "That can be a very effective strategy, but it's not the only one. It's not the only motivation. The people who tend to do really well at Amazon have more of an explorer's mentality. They're waking up in the morning, in the shower, thinking, 'What can we invent for customers?' . . . Both models can work, and you do see both models out there. [But] if you have to pick one of those two, I prefer the customer obsession to the competitor obsession. . . . The customer-obsessed culture works better when you're the leader. One of the problems that competitor-obsessed companies have is that they lose their North Star when they're number one. They have nothing to think about in the shower." And then Bezos tilted his head toward the sky and gave his jubilant, uproarious laugh.

Legere points out that a strategy that focuses on an enemy or rival needn't always focus on an *actual* enemy. Sometimes the rival can be an animating idea or concept. At Global Crossing, which spent parts of Legere's tenure teetering on the brink of bankruptcy, the idea of bankruptcy became the enemy. Other CEOs might attack ideas like "waste" or "defects" or "complacency" or "bureaucracy" with such a zeal that those ideas become full-blown enemies.

Whatever outsiders may think of Legere's approach, the data shows it is working. When Legere became T-Mobile's CEO, it had

29 million subscribers; when we met in 2016, it had 66 million. Its stock has more than doubled. Still, the CEO insists that when it comes to calling out rivals, he's just getting started. "There's tons more we can do to solve customer pain points, and the bad guys are making it easier all the time."

Chapter Seven

THE PSYCH-UP PILL

*SHOULD WHITE-COLLAR WORKERS MEDICATE
THEIR WAY TO HIGHER PERFORMANCE?*

S cott Stossel is the editor of the *Atlantic* and the author of two acclaimed books. He's a smart, accomplished guy. But when he's invited to talk about his work on television, at a conference, or at a bookstore, he is, by his own account, a complete basket case. He sweats and trembles. He gets nauseated and has trouble breathing. There's a chance he may faint.

So Stossel does what a growing number of professionals do to get through their toughest moments at work: He medicates.

His routine begins four hours before he takes the stage, when he takes a .5 milligram of the sedative Xanax. An hour before the event, he takes a second .5 milligram of Xanax and 20 milligrams of Inderal (generic name: propranolol), a beta-blocker that's become the go-to medicine for people who suffer from performance anxiety. Stossel chases the pills with a shot of vodka; he does a second shot fifteen minutes before he's due to speak.

As he stands at the podium, Stossel keeps more Xanax and a couple of minibar-sized bottles of vodka in a pocket; if he gets acutely anxious, he may discreetly pop another pill or take another drink during the event. As he recounts in *My Age of Anxiety,* a candid memoir of his disorder: "If I've managed to hit the sweet spot—that perfect combination of timing and dosage where the cognitive and psychomotor sedating effect of the drugs and alcohol balances out the physiological hyperarousal of the anxiety— then I'm probably doing okay up here; nervous but not miserable; a little fuzzy but still able to convey clarity." But some days, that equilibrium proves elusive. He often overmedicates to the point of seeming slurry; other days he undermedicates, which leaves him sweating profusely, his voice quavering, and creating the possibility that he'll run off the stage in midsentence.

While doctors probably won't applaud Stossel's use of vodka as a pre-performance aid, his use of a Xanax and a beta-blocker will stir little controversy. He's someone with an unambiguous, decades-long diagnosis of a debilitating anxiety disorder, and he's using prescribed medication under medical supervision.

Still, nearly everyone feels anxious about public speaking. The racing heartbeat, dry mouth, and sweating that commonly afflicts public speakers is so widespread as to be normal. Medicine is a tool to treat sickness, but if nearly everyone experiences some of these symptoms when approaching a lectern, can anyone who's nervous on a stage benefit from these medications?

For two of my friends, both writers, the answer is an unequivocal yes. Each of them uses beta-blockers, and they're open about it with friends, though they asked me to not use their names in this book.

By most measures, these friends are wildly successful. They've managed staffs and appeared on television. I've watched both speak easily and adeptly in public. In person, each is gregarious, funny, and charming. Neither seems anxious.

They're not the type you'd expect to need a chemical assist, but both credit the drug with transforming their careers.

The first friend, a woman in her fifties, won a public speaking competition in college. Early in her career she felt no nerves when speaking to groups of colleagues. But as she grew older, three things happened.

The first was an incident more than a decade ago. Her boss asked her on short notice to speak to a group. She was unprepared, and it went badly: She began sweating, and her voice rose to a high pitch. "It was a train wreck," she says quietly. Afterward, she began worrying it could happen again.

As her career advanced, speaking became a bigger part of her responsibilities. "There was this shift where my performance as a speaker began to have a direct effect on how people viewed me as a leader," she said. "I was representing my company, and if I did badly, it might hurt me during my annual review."

The third complication was that she wrote a best-selling book, and she began giving paid speeches. She remembers her first big one, to a group of doctors who'd flown her first class to their event. At dinner the night before her appearance, the organizers made clear that she was the event's big draw. "They hadn't just invited me to fill the hour. What I had to say was really important to them," she says, describing the enormous pressure she felt.

That's why, before the trip, she'd gone to her doctor and asked for beta-blockers. The doctor was agreeable: He'd previously prescribed them for violinists and for a professional pool player. She took the maximum dosage before the speech. "All of my bad things that usually happened—the sweating, the breathing—didn't happen," she says. "I don't know if it's psychosomatic or not, but the pills just tamp down all of the physical sensations."

Scientifically speaking, that's exactly what beta-blockers are supposed to do. Discovered by Scottish pharmacologist James Black in 1962 as a treatment for heart disease, the chemicals inhibit the body's response to adrenaline, lowering blood pressure and reducing the risk of heart attack. By the 1970s, doctors had begun using them to reduce performance anxiety, particularly in musicians. However, that remains a secondary use; beta-blockers remain primarily used to improve people's circulatory system.

For his work, Black won the Nobel Prize, and upon his death in 2010, the *New York Times* credited him with "extending the lives of millions of people."

While propranolol won't help my friend live longer, she says it has changed her life. "Now when I speak, I don't feel nervous at all, and speaking has become a really fun and lucrative part of my career," she says.

The other writer, in his forties, tells a similar story. He'd done some public speaking and TV appearances in his twenties and thirties, and he never had a problem. He didn't dread public speaking. In fact, he enjoyed it. But at one point, he had a panic attack while at a podium. So before he went on a book tour, he asked his doctor for a prescription for a beta-blocker. He takes a tiny dose, half a tablet. "It just subtracts the possibility that your body is going to rebel against you," he says.

These two friends use the medication in slightly different ways. The female writer describes getting nervous before most speeches, and she uses the medication to lessen this predictable jitteriness. In contrast, the male writer sees the pill as a safety net. He says he could probably perform without nerves nine out of ten times without the pill; he's taking the medication as a precaution against the one-in-ten chance that something might trigger a panic attack.

"The medicine helps immeasurably, and I've become an evangelist for it," he says. "It's improved my career by making me a more confident public speaker."

2.

When we think about "performance-enhancing drugs," our minds immediately go to famous athletes using banned substances to build muscles and heal faster. Lance Armstrong, Mark McGwire, Marion Jones—the list of athletes whose legacies are tainted by alleged (or, in some cases, admitted) drug use seems to grow longer every year.

But athletes aren't the only ones ingesting substances, banned or otherwise, to do their work better.

Much of this chemical enhancement is a legal and prosaic part of the daily routine. Consider caffeine, that ubiquitous energizer. Mark McLaughlin, the surgeon introduced on the first page of this book, uses it prodigiously to maintain energy during surgeries; the Yelp sales team, featured in Chapter Three, chugs Red Bull midafternoon to fuel their late-afternoon cold calls. Studies have consistently shown that caffeine increases cognitive function, alertness, and energy levels; caffeine is a potent enough performance enhancer that an athlete who has too much of it in his blood can be penalized under NCAA rules. My employer, like many, provides workers with all the coffee we care to drink, and many people have a hard time getting anything done if they don't start their day with several cups.

Similarly, many professionals signal the end of the workday

with a cocktail or two. It's counterintuitive to identify alcohol as a performance enhancer, and indeed, for the vast majority of activities, even moderate doses will diminish performance. But despite this significant potential for harm, in some situations, in carefully moderated doses, alcohol's disinhibiting qualities can be useful as a social lubricant. This is why so much business networking takes place over cocktails. My local newspaper, the *Boston Globe,* runs a weekly "Dinner with Cupid" column that chronicles a couple's blind date, and it's striking how many of these daters enjoy a solo cocktail while getting ready. There's a reason it's called "liquid courage."

Throughout history, that chemical courage has extended to the battlefield, as well. In *Shooting Up: A Short History of Drugs and War,* the Polish historian Lukasz Kamienski chronicles how a wide variety of drugs—including alcohol, opium, cocaine, and LSD—have been not only embraced by soldiers, but systematically supplied to them by officers in armies dating back to the time of Homer. Many of the drugs are stimulants, which are used, Kamienski writes, to "build stamina, provide energy, eliminate the need to sleep, combat fatigue, and reinforce the fighting spirit. They also enhance courage, improve determination, and fuel aggression." Between battles, soldiers use downers such as alcohol to deal with the stress and trauma of combat. Kamienski argues that the use of mind-altering substances makes sense given the existential dilemma at the heart of combat: Though humans have an inborn instinct for self-preservation, soldiers are routinely forced to march *toward* situations that increase their risk of death. Given that dynamic, Kamienski writes, "Wouldn't it actually be astonishing if the military had not reached for pharmacological support?"

For white-collar workers, for decades the king of high-powered enhancers has been amphetamines. The first synthetic amphetamine was patented by a chemist named Gordon Alles, and it went on the market in 1932 as an over-the-counter inhaler called Benzedrine; a few years later, the drug became available in pill form. (Alles was an unusually prolific chemist: A few years after developing amphetamines, he created the related chemical compound MDMA, better known as ecstasy.) Amphetamines work by increasing levels of the neurotransmitters dopamine and norepinephrine; this serves to inhibit drowsiness, improve concentration, reduce hyperactivity, and reduce symptoms of depression. In reading the history of amphetamines, originally marketed to ease sinus congestion, it's striking just how quickly people began identifying other beneficial uses. By 1946, amphetamines were used to treat thirty-nine distinct clinical problems, including epilepsy, Parkinson's disease, schizophrenia, alcoholism, narcosis, opiate addition, bed-wetting, migraines, depression, irritable colon, and radiation sickness.

As soon as the little pills hit pharmacy shelves, amphetamines emerged as the first widely used "cognitive enhancer," taken by otherwise healthy people to help them think more sharply for longer periods of time. Jazz musicians took it to enable them to play longer sets. Beat Generation writers downed the heart-shaped green and orange pills; Jack Kerouac wrote *On the Road* during a three-week-long amphetamine binge. Doctors recognized the downsides of amphetamine use, which include psychosis, addiction, and death. Many people kept taking them anyway. "Despite a rising increase in adverse publicity and growing reports of potential addiction, Americans continued their love affair with amphetamines," writes Elaine Moore in her history of the drug. "Students, professors, artists, musicians, medical personnel, truck drivers, athletes, writers, and actors became some of amphetamines' biggest fans." Moore, a medical technologist and health writer, recalls that the drug was so commonplace that when she was in college in the late 1960s, she used it herself to study for exams. In response to the dangers, amphetamines became more tightly regulated during the 1970s, which may have inadvertently led to the increasing popularity of cocaine.

By then, a new set of drugs used to treat a new kind of condition was taking their place. Since the 1930s, researchers had observed that stimulants have a beneficial effect on "behavioral-disordered" schoolchildren, and by the early 1960s pharmacologists had created the amphetamine variant methylphenidate, better known by its trade name: Ritalin. The underlying condition the drug was used to treat is not new: The first written description by a doctor of a child suffering from poor attention, focus, and impulse control dates to the sixteenth century. But during the 1960s, psychologists began paying more attention to the problem of "hyperactive" children, and using medication to treat them. By the 1990s, the conventional wisdom that children simply "outgrew" the condition in adolescence waned, and the number of people (including adults) taking stimulants to treat it increased. By 2014, according to the Centers for Disease Control, just over 10 percent of American children ages five to seventeen had been diagnosed with ADHD. The good news for these children is that drugs like Ritalin and Adderall are generally effective in treating the condition.

As with earlier generations of amphetamines, however, usage expanded beyond people prescribed to use them to treat a malady. The prevalence of unprescribed Ritalin and Adderall use remains the subject of much debate. Some studies of college students have suggested that up to one third are cadging the drugs from roommates or friends, and a 2016 study found that even though prescriptions of Adderall had remained flat in recent years, the number of people ages eighteen to twenty-five who reported taking it without a prescription (meaning they obtained it improperly from someone else) had increased 67 percent. Others suggest the problem of Adderall and Ritalin abuse is overhyped by the media. One 2015 study published in the *Journal of Attention Disorders* found that less than 5 percent of Americans aged eighteen to forty-nine had utilized drugs like Ritalin or Adderall for nonmedical use. Studies examining rates of usage in Europe similarly show low-single-digit numbers.

No matter how high or low the numbers, the alleged epidemic of unprescribed stimulant use has prompted concerns not only about risks and side effects, but about basic fairness. Writing in the *New Yorker,* Margaret Talbot describes becoming interested in cognitive enhancers after learning that a young colleague competing against her at work was using a prescription stimulant to pull all-nighters to work on stories. In her article, Talbot hits the points that are common in the debate over cognitive-enhancing drugs. These stories cite an "arms-race aspect" to the pharma-fueled competitive landscape. She raises the specter of parents drugging young children to perform better in school. Talbot writes: "This may be leading to a kind of society I'm not sure I want to live in: a society where we're even more overworked and driven by technology than we already are, and where we have to take drugs to keep up; a society where we give children academic steroids along with their vitamins."

That unpleasant vision notwithstanding, the more one reads about performance-enhancing drugs, the more one can't help but wonder: How much difference would they make in how I work and perform? Writing on the Web site *Slate,* the journalist Joshua Foer describes how, intrigued by tales of Adderall's properties as a performance enhancer, he consulted with a half dozen psychiatrists to assess the risks of taking the drug himself. The consensus: Used occasionally at low dose with no contraindicating conditions, it's "probably harmless."

So he tried it for a week. "The results were miraculous," Foer writes. He achieved his best ever score on an online anagrams game. He read 175 pages of a dense text. "It was like I'd been bitten by a radioactive spider," he writes, describing his unflagging productivity. "When I tried writing on the drug, it was like I had a choir of angels sitting on my shoulders. I became almost mechanical in my ability to pump out sentences. The part of my brain that makes me curious about whether I have new e-mails in my inbox apparently shut down. Normally, I can only stare at my computer screen for about 20 minutes at a time. On Adderall, I was able to work in hourlong chunks. I didn't feel like I was becoming smarter or even like I was thinking more clearly. I just felt more directed, less distracted by rogue thoughts, less day-dreamy. I felt like I was clearing away underbrush that had been obscuring my true capabilities."

However, Foer also describes feeling less creative while on Adderall—as if he's thinking with blinders on. He recounts all the potential downsides of taking the drug, a list that includes insomnia, the risk of arrest for possessing it without a prescription, and becoming physically or psychologically dependent on it. He admits to taking a pill before writing the *Slate* article. While he stops short of guaranteeing he won't take it again, he suggests he's disinclined to take it in the future.

3.

In the early 2000s, Dave Asprey was juggling a full-time job at a start-up with a nearly full-time course load as an MBA student at the Wharton School. He was struggling. "My brain wasn't working right," he says. He ended up seeing a psychiatrist and a psychologist; the former did a scan of his brain. The doctors wanted to prescribe Adderall, but after doing some research, Asprey suggested the doctor also write him a second script for modafinil, an antinarcolepsy drug that was approved by the FDA in 1998.

Modafinil is sold by the pharmaceutical company Cephalon under the brand name Provigil; originally intended as a treatment for narcolepsy, it was subsequently approved for treating sleep apnea and sleep disorders caused by shift work. It's the drug that Mark McLaughlin, the neurosurgeon in the introduction, said some of his colleagues take to stay alert during late-night surgery. Until my conversation with McLaughlin, I'd never even heard of the drug. I'm not alone: the psychologist Dave Asprey consulted had to Google it. But the psychiatrist wrote him a prescription and told him to try both drugs and report back.

Asprey hated Adderall. "It's a really harsh drug. It's not good for you," he says. Modafinil, on the other hand, worked wonderfully. "Modafinil makes it a lot easier to do whatever you need to do," Asprey says. The drug helped him stay focused and energetic. Asprey completed his MBA program; his start-up became successful and was acquired, with Asprey's personal stake worth $6 million. "Modafinil saved my career and got me through school," he says now. "I took it just about every day for eight years."

Modafinil is not an amphetamine. The drug was invented in France in the 1970s, and it's not precisely clear how it works, but it's proven to affect chemicals in the brain to increase alertness and ward off sleepiness. Like amphetamines, modafinil increases dopamine levels, but this effect is smaller, leading researchers to conclude that modafinil creates a lower risk for abuse. (It also doesn't cause the same level of jitteriness.) The drug has been tested repeatedly in military settings—both in pilots and ground troops—in studies in which the soldiers are deprived of sleep for periods extending to sixty-four hours, given different types of drugs, and subjected to cognitive tests. The drug's inventor, a French sleep researcher named Michel Jouvet, once boasted that modafinil "could keep an army on its feet and fighting for three days and nights with no major side-effects." By 2008, the tech writer Michael Arrington had identified it as a popular drug among Silicon Valley entrepreneurs. In 2013, *New York* magazine labeled it "Wall Street's new drug of choice." ABC News called it "Viagra for the Brain." On the Internet, testimonials piled up at biohacking Web sites.

Users describe the drug as making them feel unusually "crisp" and "alert." They describe marathons of work—all-night programming or writing jags—without the decrease in quality that typically comes from working long hours. Their descriptions closely track what the psychologist Mihaly Csikszentmihalyi describes as "flow": "that state in which people are so involved in an activity that nothing else seems to matter; the experience itself is so enjoyable that people will do it even at great cost, for the sheer sake of doing it."

The drug has been studied for two decades. The most comprehensive review, a 2015 metastudy that looked at twenty-four placebo-controlled tests conducted on healthy, non-sleep-deprived subjects from 1990 to 2014, tested how people performed simple tests of attention, executive function, memory, and creativity, as well as more complex tasks. The results, particularly on the more complex tasks, showed that the drug helped people perform better in most areas, with no adverse effect on mood and only rare, minor side effects. The researchers concluded: "Modafinil may well deserve the title of the first well-validated pharmaceutical 'nootropic' agent." (A "nootropic" is a drug that enhances cognitive function.)

The 2015 study created a new round of publicity. "Should you take [modafinil] to get a raise?" asked the *Atlantic.* Writer Olga Khazan didn't exactly answer that, but the evidence seemed to lean toward yes. Studies show no safety concerns, she reports, and there seems a strong consensus that modafinil is safer than amphetamines like Adderall or Ritalin. "Millions of people take [modafinil] . . . and yet, investment bankers and corporate lawyers aren't dropping dead at their desks." She asks: If this drug is as safe as existing research seems to suggest, should anyone be able to take it—and someday, will companies even encourage employees to take pills that allow them to work harder?

Since first trying the drug more than a decade ago, Asprey has emerged as its most outspoken advocate. Modafinil is just one of the many "biohacks" Asprey has used to improve his life; he's best known as the creator of the best-selling *Bulletproof Diet,* which espouses adding a special kind of butter to one's morning coffee. (He also takes handfuls of specialized vitamin supplements.) Asprey's biography says he lost a hundred pounds, gained substantial IQ points, and reduced his biological age on the regimen. Today he oversees a large empire selling supplements and advice on taking them. If you Google the word modafinil, the second and third hits (after its Wikipedia entry) are on Asprey's

Web site, and the comments section of his Web site are filled with referrals to overseas Web sites where people can buy the drug without a prescription. (When I asked him if he profits from hawking the drug, Asprey insisted, "I've never made a penny from any modafinil seller, nor from marketing it.")

His enthusiasm for the drug is unabashed. When I tell him I've seen a press report that President Obama may have taken modafinil on overseas trips, Asprey responds simply, "He's stupid if he doesn't. If you're the leader of the free world and you're going overseas and you can take something that absolutely eliminates jet lag, how could you with any sense of moral responsibility *not* take that drug?"

Asprey is disdainful of people who cite ethical reasons for not using a cognitive enhancer. Leveraging technology to perform better is what humans have done for centuries, and instead of criticizing early adopters, it's more appropriate to look askance at the Luddites who are abstaining and ask them why they're voluntarily performing at a subpar level. If I were typing this book on an old-timey typewriter, you'd think I was a kook—and Asprey sees people who object to drugs like modafinil in the same light. "I'm not sure why this isn't okay in some people's books," Asprey says. "Is using fire to stay warm 'cheating'? I think it's a vestigial effect of living in a society that was founded by Puritans. There's no rational reason to say a pharmaceutical that offers quality-of-life benefits isn't okay. Yes, there are risks with modafinil, but they're in line with the risks from a drug like ibuprofen"—which is to say, minimal.

Asprey is a smart and successful guy, but there is a huckster-ish quality that makes me leery of his testimonials. (For weeks after I speak with him, my Web browser keeps delivering ads for his proprietary Brain Octane oil.) In any case, Asprey says he doesn't regularly take mondafinil anymore. His diet and supple-ment regimen have made it largely unnecessary, he says. But he does keep a tablet in his backpack. He feels better knowing it's there if he needs it.

4.

One winter evening I'm sitting in the crowded waiting room of a medical office. I'm here to see a certified nurse specialist, and I've brought a shopping list. By now I've heard enough secondhand praise for the wonders of performance-enhancing drugs. It's time to try them for myself.

The nurse opens her door. I enter and sit in a chair under-neath her framed diplomas. She taps a digital tablet throughout. She asks for my biographical information—name, address, em-ployer, insurance. Then she delivers the classic opening line: "So what brings you here today?"

I tell her the truth: That I've come to refill a prescription for a sleeping pill, and I'm hoping to try two more medications.

I begin by asking for a refill for a sleeping pill I take sporadically for insomnia. The nurse proceeds through a lengthy discussion of my overall health, my family history, my emotional well-being, all the while tapping my information into her tablet.

When she asks about my professional life, I tell her that I spend most days writing and editing, but that my job does require occasional public speaking. In my thirties, my job required periodic appearances on television; although this is rare in my current job, it still happens once in a while. When it does, I experience the classic markers of performance anxiety: the dry mouth, the tight throat, and the rapid heartbeat. When my kids have seen me on TV, they've teased me about compulsive blinking. I tell the nurse about my friends who take beta-blockers before speeches. "They say it takes the physical signs of nervousness off the table, and it's made a big difference in their careers," I say.

The nurse nods approvingly. She's had patients who've had great results with propranolol. In fact, she suddenly scowls and looks annoyed. Earlier that morning, she'd seen a patient who was distressed because she'd become extremely nervous during a job interview. In retrospect, the nurse says she wishes she'd recommended propranolol, and she makes a note to call the patient to discuss it. It's appears she'd be happy to prescribe me this drug.

I nudge the conversation toward the next item on my list. I'm nearing the end of a book project, I explain. Although I've written books before, I find myself unusually distracted lately. I'm multitasking, and checking my phone, e-mail, and social media too much. There are days when I'm not as focused as I should be. I've read about a drug called modafinil that helps improve attention. I wonder if I'd benefit from it.

She seems skeptical. She explains that modafinil is typically used to treat sleep narcolepsy or specific sleep problems caused by shift work. Since neither of those situations apply to me, she says, this would be off-label usage, and she's not sure if my insurance plan would cover it.

I emphasize that I don't want to try anything unsafe. But I explain that for the next few months, as I rush to meet the book deadline, I will be putting in a second shift some evenings to finish the book. "I'm definitely not looking for a pill I'd take every day. I'd only be looking to use it on a handful of days, when I want to be really focused and productive," I say.

She's listening, but she's also playing with her tablet. I realize she's still focused on the question of whether my insurance would cover modafinil. I tell her I'm not very worried about the cost. Really, how expensive could it be? She taps a few buttons. "It looks like it costs $923 for a thirty-day supply," she says. *Yikes.* I gulp, but tell her I'm more worried about whether the drug is medically safe for me. At this point in the conversation, I'm guessing she will decline to prescribe me modafinil.

I've misread her. "Actually, from a medical standpoint I'd be more concerned about the side effects of the beta-blocker," she says, since that drug can cause light-headedness and drops in blood pressure. She feels both drugs are safe. She talks about the need to try a small dose of the beta-blocker at a time when I'm not speaking in public, to get a sense of how my body handles it before I take it in an actual high-pressure situation. I shouldn't take either with too much caffeine or with any alcohol.

As we wind down our discussion, she uses her tablet to send two prescriptions to my local CVS. When I go to pick up the pills the next day, I brace myself for a gargantuan bill. In fact, my insurance covers it; my total co-pay for thirty tablets each of propranolol and modafinil is fourteen dollars, and each script is renewable three times.

5.

A few days later, on President's Day, I drive a half hour to the college I attended and take up residence in the university library. At just after 10 A.M., I take my first 100-milligram tablet of modafinil.

Let's stipulate up front that from an experimental standpoint, this is an extremely poor design, the antithesis of a double-blind controlled study. I've read a lot about the effectiveness of this drug, so the odds of a placebo effect are quite high. I *want* it to work and believe it will. I'm also trying it in a college library—a place where I love to write, and one where I'm unusually focused and productive.

Even without the pharmaceutical aid, I'd probably get a lot

done today, so it's hard to say how much better I'd work while taking modafinil. Nonetheless, after taking the pill, I worked steadily with few breaks for eleven hours. I am less distracted and more focused. I'm in a state of flow. My sense of time feels different; I'm working so steadily that hours pass quickly. By the end of that stretch, I feel much less tired than I would ordinarily be. When I pack up my briefcase to go home, I feel like if I wasn't obligated to get a good night's sleep before work the next morning, I probably could have put in a few more hours.

The side effects are minimal. At times I'm slightly more aware of my heartbeat. My appetite seems slightly diminished. But that's it.

I take modafinil a half dozen times over the next few months. It never seems quite as effective as it did that first day, for reasons I can't explain. I take it once at my magazine job, and while I'm marginally more focused, the effect is less remarkable amid the distractions of my open cubicle than it had been in the library. During another ten-hour day at the library, I notice that while my brain feels alert, the modafinil does nothing to alleviate other signs of physical tiredness—the sore back, arms, shoulders that come from spending long hours in a chair working on a keyboard. This noncognitive fatigue serves as a limit on my marathon work sessions. After another long and productive workday while using modafinil, I sleep horribly and have unusually vivid dreams; afterward, I'm a little reluctant to try it again.

My modafinil test-drives go better than my attempt to use propranolol. A few weeks after I'd obtained my new prescription, I'm scheduled to moderate a panel discussion before an audience of seventy-five people at a conference. The event takes place on a Thursday. On Monday and Tuesday, I do a trial run with my beta-blocker, taking 10 milligrams with no discernable effect. On Wednesday, I manage to leave the pills in my car at the airport. I moderate the panel without the drugs. I've drafted lots of questions and done a prep call with the panelists in advance, so I'm not particularly nervous, and it goes fine.

As I wait for my next opportunity to try propranolol, one Sunday evening I get a text from a close friend. He's six months into a big job at a large corporation. On Tuesday morning, he's making a two-hour solo presentation to the CEO—a well-known figure I've read about in business magazines—to outline his strategy to turn around a flagging division. Although he's been in large meetings with the CEO, this will be their first substantive one-on-one interaction, and he's worried. He's heard of new executives who've been terminated after botching their first presentation to this CEO. "I've done tons of public speaking, and usually nerves aren't a problem," my friend said. "I'm well prepared, but I'm really anxious. The stakes are so high." In particular, he's worried about breaking into a sweat, which has happened a couple of times previously when he's been really nervous.

He cuts to the chase. "You know those pills you were telling me about for performance anxiety? Can I grab some from you before I get on the plane tomorrow?"

I say no. Although I'm not a lawyer, I suspect that sharing the prescription medication would be illegal. But he keeps after me. "Come on, hook a brother up." I want to help, but beyond the legal issues, I'm worried about the moral responsibility if he has a bad reaction to the pills. There's not enough time for him to consult his doctor: It's a Sunday night, and he leaves for the airport at 6:20 A.M. the next morning.

I come up with a compromise. "Okay, I'll drop some pills off late tonight," I tell him. Then I drive to CVS and spend ten minutes scanning the vitamin aisle, looking at pill colors and shapes to determine which vitamin could most plausibly pass for a prescription medicine. I buy a bottle of Vitamin B12, and leave five tablets in an envelope taped to his door. I text him careful instructions: Take one pill ninety minutes before the presentation, and another fifteen minutes beforehand if he still feels nervous.

The next morning he texts me from the plane: "What is this medication called?" "Propranolol," I lie. He Googles it and starts reading online reviews. "Wow, people really rave about this stuff," he says.

On Tuesday, I text him: "How did it go?" "Really well," he replies. "Those pills are magic."

Later, we debrief by phone. The primary reason the presentation went well—I can't emphasize this enough—is because he'd spent weeks preparing for it and he has excellent presentation skills. Still, he believes the pills made a difference. "I'm not sure I could have gotten through it without the medicine," he says. Knowing (or rather, thinking) that there was medicine to counteract the possibility of a quavering voice or a sweaty brow helped him relax . . . and of course, relaxing dramatically reduced the odds of a quavering voice or a sweaty brow.

Within two weeks of that first CEO presentation, he's visited his doctor and obtained his own script for propranolol.

I only hope the real drug works as well as the vitamins.

6.

My friend's wife is upset. She thinks taking propranolol before his presentation is cheating, no different than if an Olympic athlete used a performance-enhancing drug. "You're going to get addicted. You won't be able to do a presentation without it," she warns him. She also sees taking the medication as a sign of weakness. "What would you think if you found out someone reporting to you was taking an antianxiety medication before meeting with you?" she says.

My wife isn't happy either. She knows I've taken modafinil a few times, and she doesn't approve. "Do you really want people to know you're using drugs to do better at work?" she asks. "Is that the message you want to send to your kids as they look ahead to college?"

Other questions come to mind. What's the line between using these drugs and abusing them? Just because it's possible to convince a medical professional with a prescription pad that you need this drug, does that make it acceptable to use it? To what extent are prescription drugs intended only to fix a problem versus to "enhance" the life of a healthy person?

These are hardly new questions. In the stacks of the college library where I first tried modafinil, there are shelves of books that look not only at this broad issue, but also at how it applies to specific drugs. (Examples include *Listening to Prozac, Talking Back to Ritalin, The Adderall Empire,* and so on.)

A deep discussion of the ethics of biohacking and pharma-powered cognitive enhancement are beyond the scope of this book; there are already plenty of books on that subject. But I have sampled this literature. Based on what I've read, my thoughts keep returning to three points:

First, there are smart people who make a strong case for letting many more people gain easy access to cognitive-enhancement drugs. In an extreme example of this, the University of Richmond philosophy professor Jessica Flanigan wrote a 2013 journal article titled "Adderall for All: A Defense of Pediatric Neuroenhancement," in which she argued that pediatricians should be open to prescribing the medication to every child regardless of whether he or she qualifies for an ADD/ADHD diagnosis. She compares the use of these drugs to elective cosmetic surgery. Expanding legal, doctor-supervised access to these stimulants would also erode the black market, nonprescribed use that some critics believe is pervasive, particularly on college campuses. I don't find Flanigan's arguments convincing, but they are proof that the case for expanded access isn't limited to self-experimenters like Dave Asprey; in fact, this group includes people who've built careers studying and teaching at the intersection of medicine and ethics.

Second, even if you think you know where you stand on this question, medical ethicists can find new angles that make you second-guess your stance. For instance, in a 2014 journal article on the ethics of modafinil, Julie Tannenbaum asks a series of thought-provoking questions. If the primary purpose of modafinil is to let people work or study for longer hours, does it make a difference what kind of work they're doing? Although most anecdotal accounts depict white-collar knowledge workers popping the pills to get ahead in their careers or make more money, what if the work involved is drudgery, and what if bosses coerce workers to take the drug? Or what if the person taking modafinil is a research scientist, and what if by working longer hours she's able to achieve some larger, selfless goal, such as curing cancer?

Tannenbaum also challenges the conventional thinking that the primary benefits of modafinil accrue in our professional lives. What if, by reducing our need for sleep, the drug allows us to spend more of our waking times engaged in hobbies, spending quality time with loved ones, going to museums, or learning to play the piano? Tannenbaum writes: "This brings us to a key potential advantage of modafinil . . . more free time, i.e. time free from work. While modafinil does not extend how long one lives, it does increase the amount of time spent awake and thus is a form of life expansion. Moreover, the expanded time can occur when one's mind and body are in their prime, as opposed to merely adding time on at the end of one's life." Instead of viewing modafinil as part of a dystopian world in which people work all the time, what if it's a part of a utopian future in which humans "waste" less of their lives with their face in a pillow and have more time for life's out-of-the-office pleasures?

The third issue that comes up as I read these treatises: Are we drawing too fine a line between pharmaceutical enhancement and nonpharmaceutical enhancement? While this chapter has focused on two prescription drugs that can help people perform better, there is a large industry of vitamins and herbal supplements that many believe have similar effects. Is there an ethical or moral difference between using some "stack" of vitamins or nutrients versus using modafinil, simply because FDA officials have decided the latter requires a prescription and can be covered by insurance? If there is, where is the bright line?

It's a question I ponder one day when I receive an e-mail from a company called Liquifusion, which markets intravenous vitamin injections intended to increase alertness, energy, or even sexual potency. "Intravenous therapies, though previously only used by athletes and celebrities, are now available to all," the company's PR person writes. "I would love to invite you for a complimentary Liquifusion IV." She's even willing to send someone to shoot me up at my home or office. (I pass.) Is swallowing a prescription pill any better or worse than injecting energy-enhancing vitamins? For me, it's hard to say.

For my part, I'm comfortable keeping my stash of propranolol handy for rare TV or speaking appearances. I'm not completely ruling out the idea of taking modafinil, but I hope and expect to use it extremely rarely, if at all. My perspective on this has been strongly influenced by my wife bringing up the image of my children using a drug to help them study. We've always discouraged them from working past midnight on homework, arguing that if they stay on top of their work and plan ahead, there is rarely any reason to pull an all-nighter. If they're consistently falling so far behind in a class, they need to talk to the teacher to find out if they're doing something wrong, or determine if they aren't cut out for the class in the first place.

The same should be true for me. While it's natural to go through a busy period that requires a short sprint of extraordinary work, I don't want to be working fourteen hours a day on a consistent basis. If I find myself regularly needing modafinil to get ahead at work, it's probably a sign that I need to rethink the number of commitments I'm taking on, or otherwise tweak the demand side of the equation, instead of trying to chemically enhance the supply side of my labor.

But on a warm summer night in August, these lofty thoughts go out the window. I'm playing in a two-day, twenty-man annual golf tournament, a bragging-rights, trash-talk event with local friends. I'm by far the worst golfer in the group, and in our first day of competition on Friday, I'd played terribly, even by my low standards. All afternoon I'd felt nervous, especially on my tee shots, and I was continually sculling balls into the rough.

At a group dinner that night, I'm moping. Commiserating with a friend across the table who's aware of my book project, I say half jokingly: "I really could have used some beta-blockers today."

It turns out this friend takes beta-blockers before important work presentations, and he has his own doctor-prescribed supply of propranolol in his travel bag. Since he knows I have a prescription of my own, he's willing to share. The next morning at the driving range, he hands me a plastic bag with two pills. I pop one before we tee off. On the tee, I feel unusually calm and confident. I'm the complete opposite of the previous day, hitting the ball rock solid. Thanks to the strokes allotted to me because of my handicap, I win a couple of holes early on; on the ninth hole, I hit a high-pressure putt to put my team ahead on the front nine. My playing partner, a much better golfer, can't hit his stride, and I'm left carrying our team. With the chemical assistance, I'm able to rise to the challenge.

By the afternoon, with the meds wearing off, my putting skills diminish. I once again card the worst score among the twenty players. Our ten-man team loses, but my partner and I had a shot at winning our match up until the sixteenth hole. "Dan played out of his mind today," my opponent announces as the teams gather for postround drinks. Apparently there's a reason the PGA has outlawed the use of beta-blockers.

Since I'm not a PGA player, those rules don't apply to me— and after this nerve-free performance, I now keep a bottle of the magic pills in my golf bag.

EPILOGUE

On my oldest child's sixteenth birthday, not long after I began writing this book, I engaged in a parental rite of passage: I drove her to the Registry of Motor Vehicles so she could obtain her learner's permit. To get it, she'd need to pass a 25-question multiple-choice test about traffic rules. She was a little nervous. So I gave her a pep talk.

"You'll do great," I said. "Remember, you only need to get eighteen questions right, so even if you don't know seven answers, you'll still pass." I paused, trying to think of what else to say. "Did you know that 85 percent of people pass the first time?" I said. (That was a lie: I had no idea what the real number is, but I thought the fake stat sounded comforting.) Finally, I resorted to focusing on the minor consequences if she can't find her way through this thicket: "Even if you fail, we'll come back next week and you can take it again."

Although I didn't know it at the time, psychologists have a term for this ass-backward approach to pre-performance motivation. It's called "defensive pessimism," a fancy term for my tendency to try to psych up my children by presenting them with the worst-case-scenario and then explaining why, even if that happens, things won't be so bad.

If you've read this far, I hope you realize this isn't an optimal approach. It primes the recipient to think about failure, when instead you should be reminding them of their strengths, reviewing the strategic plan, and building up their confidence.

I don't give this type of pep talk anymore. It's just one of the changes I made after learning the lessons contained in this book.

I hope the preceding chapters have led you to make some modifications to your pre-performance routine, as well. Although *Psyched Up* isn't intended to be an explicit self-help book, I hope it's helped you think critically about how you should best spend the final moments before you perform and about the techniques that work best for you.

To help you in this process, as a final step, I want to do a quick inventory of the tools I've added to my pre-performance tool kit as a result of writing this book.

It goes without saying: Not every technique will work for everyone. I haven't learned to do the centering exercise outlined in

Chapter One. (I prefer the reappraisal technique, telling myself that I'm excited rather than nervous.) I rarely utilize trash talk or rivalry. Since I don't lead a team at work, my pep talks are limited to my kids, who mostly ignore me.

Other techniques in this book have become part of my repertoire. Although I don't use a custom audio sound track like the lacrosse players at West Point, I do try to boost my confidence before I perform by rereading a piece of my best writing, or listening to an old radio interview in which I was unusually articulate. Following Gary Latham's advice, my office wall is filled with images of my most successful magazine stories. In certain circumstances, I find beta-blockers to be a useful way to combat nerves.

At the gym, I'm more aware of what music I listen to before and during workouts. For cognitive work like writing, I've learned that as an introvert who prefers quiet, no sound track can help me as much as blissful silence—so I've traded my playlists for earplugs and industrial-style soundproof headphones.

And while I don't use it often, I still have Malcolm Gladwell's lucky keyboard sitting on a table in my office, in case I need it.

It's also useful to think about when and how often you'll use your own set of techniques. Recall Stanley McChrystal's wisdom about pep talks: He rarely used them with Special Forces who were doing three missions a night, because using any tool that frequently will necessarily diminish its power. The same is true for most tools discussed in this book. They will be most effective if you refrain from using them every day, and instead reserve them for those select days when your performance makes a meaningful difference in your life and career.

It's fitting to end this book by reemphasizing something I said in the beginning: that there's no substitute for focused practice, and lots of it. Getting psyched up is something you layer on top of actual rehearsal, with the goal of giving you a small boost and an incremental advantage.

In our performance-oriented culture, those small boosts can make a big difference.

Acknowledgments

This book wouldn't exist if I hadn't spent the last few years immersed in academic research as an editor at the *Harvard Business Review*. I'm fortunate to have this job, and to have had bosses—Adi Ignatius, Amy Bernstein, Sarah Cliffe, and Christina Bortz—who are supportive of my outside writing. I am also indebted to *HBR* colleagues Amy Meeker, Martha Spaulding, and Susan Donovan for their skillful assistance with my editing duties, and to Karen Dillon for helping me get hired.

Sarah Rainone consulted on the proposal for this book. Rena Kirsch did early research. Matt Mahoney provided crucial fact-checking. Jane Cavolina copyedited the manuscript and brought coherence to the endnotes. Mark Starr, David Kaplan, Amy Meeker, Dean Streck, and Chris Bersani read and commented on portions of the manuscript.

Tim Sullivan read the entire manuscript and provided vital guidance throughout the project. My debts to him run deep.

For assistance in suggesting sources, reporting ideas, or other support, thanks to Adam Bryant, Brad Stone, John Carter, Colleen Carter, Frank Cespedes, Mark Roberge, David Kaplan, Nate Zinsser, Adam Rogers, David Lefort, Brooke Hammerling, Alison Beard, Scott Berinato, N'Gai Croal, Marc Peyser, Rafi Mohammed, Keith Ferrazzi, Keith Naughton, Christian Megliola, Stefani Finks, Dave Lievens, Susannah Meadows, Matt West, Craig Nichols, Mark McNamara, Ed Crowley, Eben Harrell and Eddie Yoon.

Thanks to the many publicists who helped to arrange interviews, and to the dozens of experts whom I interviewed but did not quote or refer to in the text. I appreciate the time and insights these people shared.

Special thanks to the U.S. Military Academy at West Point, IMG Academy, and The Julliard School for providing access to their campuses and personnel.

Several high school teammates offered reflections on how our 1980s pregame athletic routines translate to professional life; Eric Riso and Andy Bordick were especially insightful.

Thanks to Francis Storrs, Susanne Althoff, and Veronica Chao at the *Boston Globe Magazine*. I have learned much about public speaking from Nitin Nohria, Brian Kenny, and Jean Cunningham, and I am fortunate to work with them.

At Portfolio, special thanks to Adrian Zackheim, Will Weisser,

Tara Gilbride, Maria Gagliano, Victoria Miller, Chris Sergio, Vivian Roberson, and Kaushik Viswanath.

Eric Nelson edited this book with energy and enthusiasm. The manuscript emerged from his computer smarter, better organized, and more concise. I appreciate his hard work and good humor.

Rafe Sagalyn, my agent, immediately saw the potential in this idea. I am lucky to have him guiding me through the publishing world.

I'm very fortunate to have my parents and in-laws, and sister and brothers-in-law, to talk over ideas and offer encouragement.

My longstanding curiosity about how people get psyched up before big events coalesced while watching my children tryout and compete in youth sports. Abby, Jack, and Tommy have remained (mostly) good-natured even as I've tried out pep talks and musical playlists on them. Watching them grow into accomplished performers in all areas of life has been a source of great joy.

The stress of writing books is visible in a variety of ways—longer hours at work, fewer vacations, and an increase in half-finished home improvement projects among them. My wife, Amy, tolerates these and other annoyances with grace, and I'm lucky to have her patience and love.

Notes

CHAPTER ONE: FIGHTING BACK AGAINST FIGHT OR FLIGHT

20 **doctors began injecting adrenaline:** Brian B. Hoffman, *Adrenaline* (Cambridge, Mass.: Harvard University Press, 2013).

20 **revived the animal:** Ibid., 160.

20 **perform Lazarus-like revivals:** Ibid., 72.

20 **"It increases the output":** Ibid., 15.

21 **including Paul McCartney:** Sara Solovitch, *Playing Scared: A History and Memoir of Stage Fright* (New York: Bloomsbury, 2015), 3.

22 **"both utterly mysterious":** Ibid., 2.

22 **list the techniques:** Ibid., 3.

22 **She describes the incident:** Carly Simon, *Boys in the Trees: A Memoir* (New York: Flatiron Books, 2015), 346–52.

22 **"It's terribly paradoxical":** Stephen Holden, "Carly Simon Triumphs Over Her Own Panic," *New York Times,* June 16, 1987.

23 **at a 1996 birthday performance:** John Lahr, "Petrified," *New Yorker,* August 28, 2006.

26 **talked about being "excited":** Alison Wood Brooks, "Get Excited: Reappraising Pre-Performance Anxiety as Excitement," *Journal of Experimental Psychology: General* 143, no. 3 (2013): 1144–58.

27 **calls "cognitive change":** James J. Gross, "Emotion Regulation: Current Status and Future Prospects," *Psychological Inquiry* 26, no. 1 (2015): 1–26.

29 **"appraisals of their internal states":** Jeremy P. Jamieson, Wendy Berry Mendes, Erin Blackstock, and Toni Schmader, "Turning the Knots in Your Stomach into Bows: Reappraising Arousal Improves Performance on the GRE," *Journal of Experimental Psychology* 46, no. 1 (2009): 208–12.

31 **People perform best:** Peter A. Hancock and H. C. Neil Ganey, "From Inverted U to the Extended U: The Evolution of a Law of Psychology," *Journal of Human Performance in Extreme Environments* 7, no. 1 (2003), article 3.

33 **Nideffer taught the process:** I interviewed Robert Nideffer as part of my reporting, but the description of his development of centering is drawn primarily from Don Greene's book *Fight Your Fear and Win* (New York: Broadway Books, 2001), 50.

33 **centered shooters performed significantly better:** Ibid., 51–52.

34 ***Fight Your Fear and Win:*** Ibid., 53-59.

36 **"The whole idea behind":** Ibid., 56.

CHAPTER TWO: WHY YOU NEED A PRE-PERFORMANCE RITUAL

45 **"Getting into the character":** "The 'How Does Stephen Colbert Work?' Edition," "Working" podcast, episode 1, transcript, *Slate,* October 16, 2014, www.slate.com/articles/podcasts/working/2014/ 10/stephen_colbert_on_his_improv_background_and_how_he _gets_in_character_for.html.

47 **the things Seinfeld does:** Aidan P. Moran, *The Psychology of Concentration in Sports Performers: A Cognitive Analysis* (Hove, U.K.: Psychology Press, 1996).

48 **The use of structured routines":** Stewart Cotterill, "Pre-Performance Routines in Sport: Current Understanding and Future Directions," *International Review of Sport and Exercise Psychology* 3, no. 2 (2010): 132–53.

49 *The Checklist Manifesto:* Atul Gawande, *The Checklist Manifesto: How to Get Things Right* (New York: Picador, 2009).

50 **LeBron James has a long set:** Sean D. Hamill, "For James, Game-Day Quirks Evolve into the Ritual," *New York Times*, February 11, 2010.

51 **most ritualistic player . . . Wade Boggs:** http://nowiknow.com/ superstitious-superstar/.

51 **"A solid routine":** Mason Currey, *Daily Rituals: How Artists Work* (New York: Alfred A. Knopf, 2015), xiv.

52 **overview of research into superstition:** Stuart Vyse, *Believing in Magic* (New York: Oxford University Press, 1997), 90.

54 **exam superstitions are common:** Ibid., 214.

55 **"Soon the birds were dancing":** Ibid., 71.

55 **see how activating superstitions:** Lysann Damisch, Barbara

Stoberock, and Thomas Mussweiler, "Keep Your Fingers Crossed! How Superstition Improves Performance," *Psychological Science* 21, no. 7 (2010):1014–20.

56 **"specific abilities can transfer through contagion":** Thomas Kramer and Lauren G. Block, "Like Mike: Ability Contagion Through Touched Objects Increases Confidence and Improves Performance," *Organizational Behavior and Human Decision Processes* 124 (2014), 215–28.

56 **what types of people:** Vyse, *Believing in Magic*, 55.

57 **his ninety-hour workweeks:** Nate Ryan, "Chad Knaus Sacrifices to Be NASCAR's Top Crew Chief," *USA Today*, February 21, 2014.

62 **individual rituals or group rituals:** Tami Kim, Sezer Ovul, Juliana Schroeder, Jane Risen, Francesca Gino, Michael Norton, "Group Rituals Improve Group Performance," draft manuscript.

64 **how rituals affect consumption:** Kathleen D. Vohs, Yajin Wang, Francesca Gino, and Michael I. Norton, "Rituals Enhance Consumption." *Psychological Science* 24, no. 9 (2013), 1714–721.

65 **how rituals affect how people feel:** Michael I. Norton and Francesca Gino, "Rituals Alleviate Grieving for Loved Ones, Lovers, and Lotteries," *Journal of Experimental Psychology: General*, forthcoming.

69 **the Gypsy Robe:** The Gypsy Robe ritual is described in detail at www.actorsequity.org.

70 **a "small riot":** Jim Dwyer, "Backstage at 'Lucky Guy,' a Character Watches Tom Hanks Keep the Cast Loose," *New York Times*, July 2, 2013.

71 **Critics agreed. Reviewing *The River*:** Ben Brantley, "A Reserve So Deep, You Could Drown," *New York Times*, November 16, 2014.

72 **the club had previously been owned:** Charles Lee, Sally A. Linkenauger, Jonathan Z. Bakdash, Jennifer A. Joy-Gaba, and Dennis
R. Profitt, "Putting Like a Pro: The Role of Positive Contagion in
Golf Performance and Perception," PLoS ONE 6, no. 10 (2011):
e26016.

72 **"Defend Your Research":** "You'll Golf Better If You Think Tiger
Has Used Your Clubs," *Harvard Business Review.* July–August 2012.

CHAPTER THREE: DON'T JUST WIN ONE FOR THE GIPPER

84 **"preternatural ability to fire people up":** Jennifer Reingold, "The
Secret Coach," *Fortune*, July 21, 2008.

87 **baseball managers John McGraw:** Ray Robinson, *Rockne of
Notre Dame* (New York: Oxford University Press, 1999), 62.

87 **Rockne stammered badly:** Ibid., 145.

88 **"The fact that Rockne never revealed":** Ibid., 91.

93 **completed his dissertation:** Keith Yellin, *Battle Exhortation* (Columbia: University of South Carolina Press, 2008).

93 **twenty-three "Common topics":** Ibid., 71–72.

96 **gave "an awesome speech":** Phil Bronstein, "The Shooter," *Esquire,* March 2013.

96 **"Nothing he said":** Mark Owen, *No Easy Day* (New York: Dut-
ton, 2012), 207.

97 **SEAL operators were so relaxed:** Ibid., 210.

97 **"He was driven by":** David Halberstam, *The Education of a Coach*
(New York: Hyperion, 2005), 144–45.

98 **"At that time most coaches":** Phil Jackson and Hugh Delehanty,
Eleven Rings (New York: Penguin Press, 2013).

99 **taped pregame speech to ninety soccer players:** Tiffanye M. Vargas-Tonsing and John B. Bartholomew, "An Exploratory Study of the Effects of Pregame Speeches on Team Efficacy Beliefs," *Journal of Applied Social Psychology* 36, no 4 (2006): 918–33.

99 **surveyed 151 soccer players:** Tiffanye M. Vargas-Tonsing, "An Exploratory Examination of the Effect of Coaches' Pre-Game Speeches on Athlete's Perceptions of Self-Efficacy and Emotion," unpublished working paper.

100 **found that 90 percent of players:** Tiffanye M. Vargas-Tonsing, "Athletes Perceptions of the Psychological, Emotional, and Performance Effects of Coaches' Pre-Game Speeches," *International Journal of Coaching Science* 5, no. 1 (2011): 27–43.

100 **pep talk that's information rich:** Tiffanye M. Vargas-Tonsing and Jianmin Guan, "Athletes Preferences for Informational and Emotional Pre-Game Speech Content," *International Journal of Sports Science and Coaching,* 2, no. 2 (2007), 171–80.

100 **tracked coaches' speeches across a season:** As this book went to press, Staw's basketball study remains unpublished and not publicly available.

105 **Motivating Language Theory has:** J. Mayfield, M. Mayfield, and J. Kopf, "Motivating Language: Exploring Theory with Scale Development," *Journal of Business Communication* 32, no. 4, (1995): 329–44.

CHAPTER FOUR: CREATING A PERFORMANCE PLAYLIST

114 **The Patriots fumbled:** Game recap for the New England Patriots versus Denver Broncos, November 24, 2013, obtained from www .nfl.com/gamecenter/2013112411/2013/REG12/Broncos@Patriots

#menu=gameinfo%7Ccontentld%3A0ap2000000288072&tab
=recap.

116 **single largest employer:** Bruce P. Gleason, "Military Music in the United States: A Historical Examination of Performance and Training," *Music Educators Journal* 101, no. 3 (March 2015): 37–46.

117 **two-part "synthesis and review":** Costas I. Karageorghis and David-Lee Priest. "Music in the Exercise Domain: A Review and Synthesis (Parts I and II)." *International Review of Sport and Exercise Psychology* 5. no. 1 (March 2012): 44–84.

119–20 **shown that motivational music can lead to:** Costas I. Karageorghis and Peter C. Terry. *Inside Sports Psychology* (Champaign, Ill.: Human Kinetics, 2011), 197–205.

120 **break a workout into different components:** Ibid., 216–18.

122 **two researchers asked pairs of runners:** K.G. Hall and B. Erickson. "The Effects of Preparatory Arousal on Sixty-Meter Dash Performance." *Applied Research in Coaching and Athletics Annual* 10 (1995): 70–79.

126 *New York* **magazine essay:** As told to Alexa Tsoulis-Reay. "My Wife and I Are (Both) Pregnant," *New York* magazine, January 10, 2016, nymag.com/thecut/2016/01/dual-pregnancy-c-v-r.html.

128 **music in office settings:** Anneli B. Haake, "Music Listening in UK Offices: Balancing Internal Needs and External Considerations" (PhD diss., University of Sheffield, 2010).

133 **Four minutes after:** Game recap for the Boston Red Sox versus Toronto Blue Jays, April 27, 2015, obtained from scores.espn.go.com/mlb/playbyplay?gameId=350427102.

134 **a history of the practice:** Daniel Brown, "The Secrets Behind Baseball's Walk-Up Music," *San Jose Mercury News,* June 14, 2011.

CHAPTER FIVE: THE KEYS TO CONFIDENCE

146 **Research in Athletics Laboratory:** Christopher D. Green, "Psychology Strikes Out: Coleman R. Griffith and the Chicago Cubs," *History of Psychology* 6, no. 3 (2003), 267–83.

146 **the 1926 book:** Coleman R. Griffith, *Psychology of Coaching.* New York: Scribners, 1926. 87-90.

147 **"The clash of cultures":** Green, "Psychology Strikes Out."

147 **When the San Diego Chargers:** Jean M. Williams and William F. Straub, "Sports Psychology: Past, Present, and Future," in *Applied Sports Psychology: Personal Growth to Peak Performance*, ed. Jean M. Williams (Boston: McGraw Hill, 2010), 5.

150 **more sophisticated textbook:** Jean M. Williams, ed., *Applied Sports Psychology: Personal Growth to Peak Performance* (Boston: McGraw Hill, 2010).

150 **the psychologists teach techniques:** The summaries in the sections that follow come from the relevant chapters in Williams's textbook.

156 **Kahneman describes human cognition:** Daniel Kahneman, *Thinking, Fast and Slow* (New York: Farrar, Straus and Giroux, 2011), 20–21.

158 **theories of why people choke:** Sian L. Beilock and Thomas H. Carr, "On the Fragility of Skilled Performance: What Governs Choking Under Pressure?," *Journal of Experimental Psychology: General* 130, no. 4 (2001): 701–25.

158 **"The key is":** Sian Beilock, *Choke: What the Secrets of the Brain Reveal about Getting It Right When You Have To* (New York: Atria, 2010), 76.

158 **"paying too much attention":** Ibid., 78.

160 **"the temporary activation state":** John A. Bargh and Tanya L. Chartrand, "Studying the Mind in the Middle: A Practical Guide to Priming and Automaticity Research," in *Handbook of Research Methods in Social and Personality Psychology*, ed., Harry T. Reis and Charles M. Judd (New York: Cambridge University Press, 2014), 316.

161 **words that connote "elderly":** John A. Bargh, Mark Chen, and Lara Burrows, "Automaticity of Social Behavior: Direct Effects of Trait Construct and Stereotype Activation on Action," *Journal of Personality and Social Psychology* 71, no. 2 (1996): 230–44.

162 **priming in an actual workplace:** Amanda Shantz and Gary P. Latham, "An Exploratory Field Experiment on the Effect of Subconscious and Conscious Goals on Employee Performance," *Organizational Behavior and Human Decision Processes* 109 (2009): 9–17.

162 **the results showed:** Ibid.

163 **primed with a "context-specific" photo:** Gary P. Latham and Ronald F. Piccolo, "The Effect of Context-Specific Versus Nonspecific Subconscious Goals on Employee Performance," *Human Resource Management* 51, no. 4 (July–August 2012), 511–523.

163 **how well fifty teams performed:** Gary P. Latham, "The Effect of Primed Goal on Team Performance," unpublished as of December 2015; provided by the author.

164 **"The high-power posers":** Dana R. Carney, Amy J. C. Cuddy, and Andy J. Yap, "Power Posing: Brief Nonverbal Displays Affect Neuroendocrine Levels and Risk Tolerance," *Psychological Science* 21, no. 10 (2010), 1363–68.

164 **researchers failed to find:** Andrew Gelman and Kaiser Fung,

"The Power of the 'Power Pose.'" *Slate.*, January 19, 2016, www
.slate.com/articles/health_and_science/science/2016/01/
amy_cuddy_s_power_pose_research_is_the_latest_example
_of_scientific_overreach.html.

164 **one of Cuddy's collaborators:** Jesse Singal, "'Power Posing' Co-author: 'I Do Not Believe That 'Power Pose' Effects Are
Real,'" *New York* magazine, September 26, 2016.

165 **"adopting expansive poses":** Jesse Singal and Melissa Dahl, "Here
Is Amy Cuddy's Response to Critiques of Her Power-Posing Research," *New York* magazine, September 30, 2016.

165 **asked people to write:** Joris Lammers, David Dubois, Derek D.
Rucker, and Adam D. Galinsky, "Power Gets the Job: Priming
Power Improves Interview Outcomes," *Journal of Experimental
Psychology* 49, no. 4 (2013), 776–79.

CHAPTER SIX: HARNESSING ANGER AND RIVALRY

177 **"If [Selvy] had walked":** Bob Cousy, *The Killer Instinct* (New
York: Random House, 1975), 3–5.

177 **how anger affects athletes:** Paul A. Davis, "Angry Athletes: Psychological, Physiological and Performance Implications," in *Psychology
of Anger: Symptoms, Causes, and Coping*, ed., James P. Welty (Haup-
pauge, N.Y.: Nova Science Publishers, Inc. 2011).

178 **Experimental research suggests getting angry:** Ibid.

178 **"escalating conflict, biasing perceptions":** Alison Wood Brooks,
"Emotion and the Art of Negotiation," *Harvard Business Review*,
December 2015.

180 **In cricket, they call it "sledging":** Joshua Robinson, "The Vulgar Side of Cricket," *Wall Street Journal,* December 4, 2013.

180 **radio show with Gorgeous George:** Muhammad Ali with Hana Ali, *The Soul of a Butterfly: Reflections on Life's Journey* (New York: Simon & Schuster, 2004), 71–72.

181 **"I rehearsed and planned":** Muhammad Ali with Richard Durham, *The Greatest: My Own Story* (New York: Random House, 1975), 115–16.

181 **"He entertained as much":** Robert Lipsyte, "Muhammad Ali Dies at 74," *New York Times,* June 4, 2016.

183 **In the resulting thesis:** Oliver Ben Conmy, "Investigating a Conceptual Framework for Trash Talk: Cognitive and Affective States" (masters thesis, Florida State University, 2005).

184 **players prefer to trash-talk:** Oliver Ben Comny, "Trash Talk in a Competitive Setting: Impact on Self-Efficacy, Affect, and Performance" (PhD diss., Florida State University, 2008).

184 **414 college athletes found:** David W. Rainey and Vincent Granito, "Normative Rules for Trash Talk Among College Athletes: An Exploratory Study," *Journal of Sport Behavior* 33, no. 3 (2010).

185 **Indiana University graduate student:** Stephen F. Davis, Matthew T. Huss, and Angela H. Becker, "Norman Triplett and the Dawning of Sports Psychology," *Sport Psychologist* 9 (1995), 366–75.

187 **another contestant participating simultaneously:** Norman Triplett, "The Dynamogenic Factors in Pacemaking and Competition," *American Journal of Psychology* 9 (July 1898), 507–33.

187 **"Competition spurs motivation":** Po Bronson and Ashley

Merryman, *Top Dog: The Science of Winning and Losing* (New York: Twelve, 2013), 18.

187 **the greatest teams in history:** Ibid., 205.

189 **teams play more efficient defense:** Gavin J. Kilduff, Hillary Anger Elfenbein, and Barry M. Staw, "The Psychology of Rivalry: A Relationally Dependent Analysis of Competition," *Academy of Management Journal* 53, no. 5 (2010), 943–69.

189 **featuring long-distance runners:** Gavin J. Kilduff, "Driven to Win: Rivalry, Motivation, and Performance," *Social Psychological and Personality Science* (2014).

191 **"Employees were beaten down,":** Information on how John Legere and T-Mobile utilized rivalry was obtained during an interview with Legere in May 2016. Legere subsequently wrote about this topic in an article entitled "T-Mobile's CEO on Winning Market Share by Trash-Talking Rivals" in January-February 2017 issue of *Harvard Business Review.*

192 **"profanity-spewing shock jock":** Danielle Sacks, "Who the @!#$&% IS This Guy? John Legere's Strategy for Taking New Customers by Storm," *Fast Company,* July–August 2015.

194 **he lives in:** Vivian Marino, "T-Mobile Chief Pays $18 Million for Central Park View," *New York Times,* October 16, 2015.

194 **9-square-inch temporary tattoo:** Ethan Wolff-Mann, "T-Mobile Pays $21,800 for Sponsorship Tattoo on Olympic Runner," *Time,* May 13, 2016, time.com/money/4329336/t-mobile-tattoo-nick-symmonds-olympics/.

195 **"large, multi-billion dollar":** Neeru Paharia, Jill Avery, and Anat Keinan, "Positioning Brands Against Large Competitors to Increase Sales," *Journal of Marketing Research* 51, no. 6 (2014), 647–56.

CHAPTER SEVEN: THE PSYCH-UP PILL.

202 **"If I've managed to hit"**: Scott Stossel, *My Age of Anxiety* (New York: Alfred A. Knopf, 2013), 96–97.

205 **"extending the lives"**: Lawrence K. Altman, "Dr. James Black, Pharmacologist Who Discovered Beta Blockers, Dies at 85," *New York Times*, March 22, 2010.

207 **a wide variety of drugs:** Lukasz Kamienski, *Shooting Up: A Short History of War and Drugs* (Oxford: Oxford University Press, 2016), xvii, xxiv.

208 **first synthetic amphetamine:** Elaine A. Moore, *The Amphetamine Debate* (Jefferson, N.C.: McFarland & Co., 2011), 20–21.

208 **related chemical compound MDMA:** Ibid., 22.

208 **Amphetamines work by:** Ibid., 15.

208 **used to treat thirty-nine:** Ibid., 39.

209 **Jack Kerouac wrote *On the Road*:** Ibid., 37–38.

209 **"Despite a rising increase":** Ibid., 26.

209 **the drug was so commonplace:** Ibid., 5.

209 **popularity of cocaine:** Ibid., 32.

210 **amphetamine variant methylphenidate:** Susan McCrossin, "Ritalin and Attention Deficit Disorder: History of Its Use, Effects, and Side Effects," White Paper, Learning Enhancement Center, Boulder, Colo., 1995.

210 **first written description:** Klaus W. Lange et al., "The History of Attention Deficit Hyperactivity Disorder," *ADHD Attention Deficit and Hyperactivity Disorders* 2, no 4 (2010), 241–55.

210 **taking it without a prescription:** "Adderall Misuse Rising Among Young Adults," Johns Hopkins Bloomberg School of Public

Health news release, February 16, 2016, www.jhsph.edu/news/news-releases/2016/adderall-misuse-rising-among-young-adults.html.

211 **less than 5 percent:** "Nonmedical Use and Diversion of ADHD Stimulants Among U.S. Adults Ages 18–49," *Journal of Attention Studies* 19, no. 7 (July 2015), 630–40.

211 **"This may be leading":** Margaret Talbot, "Brain Gain," *New Yorker,* April 27, 2009.

212 **"The results were miraculous":** Joshua Foer, "The Adderall Me," *Slate,* May 10, 2005, www.slate.com/articles/health_and _science/medical_examiner/2005/05/the_adderall_me.html.

214 **Like amphetamines, modafinil:** Moore, *The Amphetamine Debate,* 115–16.

214 **tested repeatedly in military settings:** Joseph V. Baranski et al., "Modafinil During 64 Hr of Sleep Deprivation: Dose-Related Effects on Fatigue, Alertness, and Cognitive Performance," *Military Psychology* 10, no. 3 (1998), 173–93.

214 **Michel Jouvet, once boasted:** Terence J. Lyons and Jonathan French, "Modafinil: The Unique Properties of a New Stimulant," *Aviation, Space, and Environmental Medicine* 62 (May 1991), 432–35.

215 **popular drug among Silicon Valley:** Michael Arrington, "How Many Silicon Valley Startup Executives Are Hopped Up On Provigil?," TechCrunch, July 15, 2008, techcrunch.com/2008/07/15/how-many-of-our-startup-executives-are-hopped-up-on-provigil/.

215 **"Wall Street's new drug":** Robert Kolker, "The Real Limitless Drug Isn't Just for Lifehackers Anymore," *New York* magazine, March 31, 2013.

215 **"Viagra for the Brain":** Dan Harris, Lana Zak, and Dr. Mark Abdel-
malek, "Provigil: The Secret to Success?," ABC News, July 17, 2012,
abcnews.go.com/Health/provigil-secret-success/story?id
=16788001.

215 **Csikszentmihalyi describes as "flow":** Mihaly Csikszentmihalyi,
Flow: The Psychology of Optimal Experience (New York: Harper-
Perennial, 1990), 4.

215–16 **Modafinil may well deserve":** R.M. Battleday and A.K. Brem,
"Modafinil for Cognitive Neuroenhancement in Healthy Non-
Sleep-Deprived Subjects: A Systematic Review," *European Neuro-
psychopharmacology* 35 (November (2015): 2101–9.

216 **"Millions of people":** Olga Khazan, "The Rise of Work Doping,"
Atlantic, August 27, 2015.

216 **the best-selling *Bulletproof Diet*:** Gordy Megroz, "Buttered
Coffee Could Make You Invincible. And This Man Very Rich,"
Bloomberg Businessweek, April 21, 2015, www.bloomberg.com/
news/features/2015-04-21/buttered-coffee-could-make-you-in
vincible-and-this-man-very-rich.

217 **President Obama may have taken:** Barbara Kantrowitz, "The
White House Mystery Drug." *Daily Beast,* May 10, 2010, http://
www.thedailybeast.com/articles/2010/03/04/the-white-house
-mystery-drug.html.

218 **The nurse opens:** While I gave the nurse practitioner a general overview of this book project when I met with her, I did
not tell her I planned to write about my own experiences using
beta-blockers or modafinil. Therefore, I chose not to name her in
the book.

226 **she argued that pediatricians:** Jessica Flanigan, "Adderall for All: A Defense of Pediatric Neuroenhancement." *HEC Forum* 25 (2013) 325.

227 **Julie Tannenbaum asks:** Julie Tannenbaum, "The Promise and Peril of the Pharmacological Enhancer Modafinil," *Bioethics* 28, no. 8 (2014), 436–45.

EPILOGUE

233 **So I gave her a pep talk:** The story about my pep talk to my daughter before her driving test previously appeared in an essay in the *Boston Globe Magazine*, "You've Been Doing Pep Talks All Wrong. Here's How to Fix Them," March 1, 2015.

Index